S0-DJM-430

Hit the Trail!

The Kids' Camping Kit

Hit the Trail!

The Kids' Camping Kit

Cecilia Dinio-Durkin and Peter Durkin

Illustrated by Rick Brown

CADER BOOKS
NEW YORK

**Andrews McMeel
Publishing**

Kansas City

To Ron
For giving us the courage to do anything and try everything—
we'll keep the campfires burning bright.   —CDD and PD

Acknowledgment
To our wonderfully insightful editor, Jackie.
Thanks for recognizing Pete's unique love for the outdoors and
giving him a chance to share it.   —CDD

Thank you for buying this Cader Book—we hope you enjoy it. And
thanks as well to the store that sold you this, and the hardworking
sales rep who sold it to them. It takes a lot of people to make a book.
Here are some of the people who were instrumental:

Editorial: Jackie Kramer, Cindy Achar, Jake Morrissey,
    Dorothy O'Brien, Polly Blair, Nora Donaghy
Design: Charles Kreloff
Copyediting/Proofing: Adaya Henis
Production: Beth Schnitzer, Tamara Haus
Legal: Renee Schwartz, Esq.

If you would like to share any thoughts about this book, or are
interested in other books by us, please write to:
Cader Books, 38 E. 29 Street, New York, NY 10016.

Or visit our web site: http://www.caderbooks.com

Copyright © 1998 Cader Company Inc., Cecilia Dinio-Durkin and Peter
Durkin. Illustrations copyright © 1998 Rick Brown. All rights reserved.
No part of this book may be used or reproduced in any manner
whatsoever without written permission of the Publisher.

Made in China

Library of Congress Catalog Card Number: 97-74521

May 1998

First Edition

10 9 8 7 6 5 4 3 2 1

Attention Schools and Businesses: Andrews McMeel Publishing books
are available for educational, business, or sales promotional use. For
information, please write to: Special Sales Department, Andrews
McMeel Publishing, 4520 Main Street, Kansas City, Missouri 64111.

Contents

● ● ● ● ● ● ● ● ● ● ● ● ● ● ● ● ● ●

Adventures Abound 48

Night Stalkings 81

Homeward Bound 90

Introduction

● ● ● ● ● ● ● ● ● ● ● ● ● ● ● ● ● ● ● ●

So you want to go camping? Who can blame you—it's not called the great outdoors for nothing! And we think it's pretty great, too. That's why we've put together our lifetime of learning in this camping book to help make your camping experience a great one.

You may be an expert camper who knows your half hitch from your clove hitch, or a first-time camper who doesn't yet know the different types of knots and their uses. Either way, this book has something for you. *Hit the Trail!* has camping and outdoors tips on everything from what and how to pack to finding and catching streamside critters and identifying constellations. We also show you how to build your own tepee, pick an edible bouquet, and make an everlasting combination journal, field guide, and scrapbook to keep a record of your trip. This book can be used before, during, and after a camping trip to help make your adventure more successful.

Whether you picture yourself sitting in a cozy campsite in the backyard, singing campfire songs and roasting marshmallows, or hiking vertical trails and pitching your tent on a ledge off the side of a mountain, you're going to have a once-in-a-lifetime experience. But before you hit the trail, play Happy Trails, the game that gives you an idea of how much you know about the outdoors. Are you a Tenderfoot, a Pioneer, or a Trailblazer? Play on, to see where you stand on your knowledge of the lay of the land!

Happy Trails

Start with question number 1 and let your answers lead you through a trail. No matter where the game sends you, you'll end up a more adventurous and knowledgeable camper.

1. **Water from a clear rushing mountain stream is**

   a. a safe source of drinking water. Go to #4.
   b. an unsafe source of drinking water. Go to #5.

2. **Oops! But don't let these questions drive you buggy; just look up the right info in this book. Then see if you can answer this:**

   While you're stargazing, if a shining object in the sky (that you're sure is not an airplane) blinks, it is most likely a
   a. star. Go to #19.
   b. planet. Go to #9.

3. **Sharpen your camping know-how by finding the correct answer in this book. But for now, find out what kind of camper you are, after answering this question:**

   When you light a fire, the best materials to use to get the flame started are
   a. split hardwood logs. Go to #12.
   b. dried up leaves, bark, or tiny twigs. Go to #16.

4. **Fast-moving water may contain bacteria that can make you very sick. Go to page 44 for more info on water. Meanwhile, try another slippery question:**

   If you are swimming during a lightning storm, be sure to
   a. get out of the water. Go to #6.
   b. stay in the water. Go to #13.

5. **Cheers to you! Now try this eye-opener:**

   The best kind of sunglasses to wear to spot fish in the water are
   a. gray polarized glasses. Go to #10.
   b. brown polarized glasses. Go to #7.

6. You're just thundering through these questions! Bet you'll think this one's for the birds!

The best thing to do if you find a baby bird on the ground is
a. take it home, since it's been abandoned by its mother. Go to #13.
b. leave it there, since its mother is probably not far away. Go to #7.

7. You are so bright! Now let's see if we can bug you with this question:

If an animal has two pairs of antennae and at least five pairs of legs, it is classified as
a. a crustacean. Go to #18.
b. an arachnid. Go to #2.

8. You're some camper! But get your head out of the clouds to answer this:

Cirrus clouds (mares' tails) are the first sign of
a. clearing weather just after a rainstorm. Go to #20.
b. continued good clear weather. Go to #11.

9. They didn't write "Twinkle, twinkle, little planet," now did they! For more cool facts about the starry sky, look on page 81. For now, wood—uh, would you answer this one?

A tepee fire
a. happens when a shelter goes up in flames. Go to #13.
b. is the shape you place logs in to build a very hot fire. Go to #12.

10. Yes, while gray polarized glasses are good, brown polarized (in our opinion) are the best. Take a look on page 66 for more fishing tips. Here's another fishy question:

While you're searching for critters in a creek, it's best to walk
a. upstream. Go to #16.
b. downstream. Go to #15.

...nd you thought that was a puff question! Look up clouds on page 50. Meanwhile, let's see how sharp you really are:

When you buy a knife, be sure to look for
a.   the biggest one you can find. Go to #3.
b.   the right knife for the job. Go to #16.

12. **Well, lookee here—a Tenderfoot! In the olden days, someone who was brave enough to hit the trail, but not experienced in the ways of the Wild West, was called a Tenderfoot. You don't know that much about camping yet, but you're eager to learn.**

13. **You didn't get this question right, but you can. Just read through the book and gather some camping info before trying this game again.**

14. **You're one hot camper! Outdoor folk who weren't afraid to try new adventures because they really knew their stuff were called Trailblazers. And that's exactly the level of camper you are!**

15. **That question just slipped away from you. But you can find out why downstream is the wrong way to go on page 62. Let's find out how much you do know about animals:**

The best time to look for wildlife is
a.   midday. Go to #3.
b.   just before sunrise and sunset. Go to #12.

16. **Just like the pioneers who set out for a new place to live, you know where you want to go and have a lot of the knowledge and means to get there. You're a Pioneer!**

17. You're very bright, but this time not quite right! For now, focus on this question:

The best way to hold binoculars is by
a. spreading your elbows as far apart as possible. Go to #2.
b. tightly tucking your elbows into your chest. Go to #8.

18. You may be able to identify crustaceans, but what about night creatures?

While using a flashlight at night, if you spot green eyes looking back at you, you've found yourself a
a. raccoon. Go to #17.
b. fox. Go to #14.

19. Remembering those nursery rhymes does come in handy, doesn't it! Here's a question that good ol' Jiminy Cricket could answer; how about you?

In most of the United States, counting the number of cricket chirps can tell you
a. how much rain to expect in the days ahead. Go to #20.
b. the current temperature. Go to #16.

20. Look on page 50, whether you wish to use clouds or animals to predict the weather. Then go to #12 to see what level of camper you are.

Getting Ready

No matter what reasons you have for exploring the great outdoors, you need to have a game plan before you can blaze any trail. Here are five questions you need to answer to help make getting ready a lot easier.

Your Action Plan

● ● ● ● ● ● ● ● ● ● ● ● ● ● ● ● ● ●

1. Where are you going?_____.
Whether you already know where you're going or you're still figuring that out, it's important to know where you want to go so you can plan your camping trip.

2. When are you going? _____.
When you're planning an outdoor trip, what you can do (and what you'll need to pack) will depend on the time of year and the weather.

3. How long will you be there?_____.
You'll need to know this to make your list of what (and how much) to bring along.

4. How will you be getting to your campsite (car, boat, bicycle, your feet)? _____.
This answer will help you decide how much you can bring and what you'll be packing your provisions in.

5. What will you be doing during your camping trip? What would you like to see or do?_____
_____
_____
_____.

Canoeing, bird-watching, rock collecting—what kind of trip is in store?

These are all important things to consider before you even start to pack. Hitting the trail without knowing the answers to these questions would be like going on a cross-country trip without a map!

Top 10 Reasons to Go Camping

10. To feed my little brother or sister to Bigfoot

9. To make s'mores

8. To build a campfire

7. Because only I can stop forest fires

6. To convince my parents I need a pocketknife

5. To find out if bears really poop in the woods

4. To answer this question: If a tree falls in the woods and no one hears it, will I make a sound if it lands on me?

3. It's the only place I can get away with wearing my coonskin cap.

2. To challenge myself

1. To experience nature, return to the simple life, and to eat s'mores!

Smart Packing

● ● ● ● ● ● ● ● ● ● ● ● ● ● ● ● ● ● ● ●

Veteran outdoor enthusiasts know that preparation is a key ingredient in a successful outdoors adventure. With the proper equipment, your camping trip is much more likely to be a success. Follow these time-tested steps to savvy packing and transform yourself into a lean, mean camping machine.

1. List the things you need (and want) to bring. Break your list into categories of clothing, food and cookware, toiletries, equipment, and special items like fishing tackle. See page 16 for a list of must-haves, plus a few handy extras to add if you've got room. Once your list is complete, mark the items as "Needs" or "Wants." If you're short on space, this will make it easier to cut nonessentials.

2. Gather the items on your list. Check them off your list as you go. Make a separate pile for each category on your list. Check to see that everything is working and in good condition. Does the flashlight have new batteries? Does your jacket still fit? Are the tent stakes there and in good shape? Make sure everything is okay before you leave home.

3. Pack. Keep everything in separate piles. Packing related items in labeled or color-coded bags or stuff sacks will make locating things easier. Squeeze all the air out of each bag before you seal it. Be sure each bag is strong enough for what it will hold. If you're hiking in to your campsite and living out of your pack, put things in heavy-duty resealable bags. If you're car camping, and have more space, put them in water-resistant bags or bins (cardboard boxes will fall apart when they're wet).

Tips for Packing a Backpack

- If you might need it in a hurry (rain poncho, camera, first-aid kit) pack it on top or in an outside pocket for easy access.
- Pack the heavy stuff in the upper middle of the pack. Distribute the weight evenly on both sides of the pack.
- Put your sleeping bag in a trash bag in the bottom of your pack to protect it from rain and to cushion the other contents.
- Roll up your clothes. Fill in spaces with little things like socks and T-shirts. Don't forget to fill up space in hollow items like boots—every square inch counts.
- If you strap stuff to the outside of your pack, check that it won't catch on branches or poke you if you sit down or fall.
- Prevent sticky situations. Wrap even the most secure plastic bottles of liquids and lotions in plastic bags.
- Don't pack glass containers. They're dangerous and a hassle when they break—and they will.
- Pack with a plan. Whenever you take something out, put it back in the same place—this way you'll always know where it is.
- Want it to stay dry? Put it in a plastic bag, which comes in handy later for dirty clothes, garbage, or recyclables.

Don't Be a Pack Rat!

Pack rats, or wood rats, collect and store just about any scraps or small objects they can carry. These critters have been known to steal coins, bottle caps, watches, keys, belt buckles, pieces of mirror—even a miner's pair of false teeth. Any object these thieves find goes right into their large nests made of sticks and lined with leaves and other soft materials. Templeton, the rat in *Charlotte's Web,* is probably the most famous pack rat of all.

Don't Leave Home Without It

• • • • • • • • • • • • • • • • • • • •

There's nothing like a huge pile of stuff towering over you to make it easy to overlook those incredibly important little items you'll be kicking yourself later for forgetting—like, say, your tent! Whenever you're packing for a camping trip, use this list (or make a copy). Make sure to add any important items you think of. Save your list; next time you go camping, you can get packed that much faster.

Another important thing to remember when you go camping is that you don't need to buy loads of expensive, high-tech equipment to have a good time. Don't scrimp when it comes to matters of safety and comfort such as a complete first-aid kit or sturdy weatherproof clothing and shelter. But remember, part of the challenge of camping is learning to make the most of what you have and being creative with the rest. Borrowing equipment is a great way to test out gear and save money. Just remember to return borrowed or rented gear in the same shape you

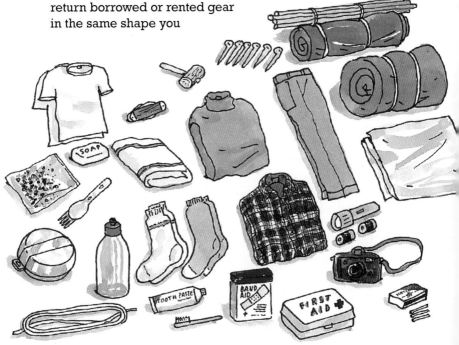

received it—it deserves the same care you'd give your own possessions.

Except in unusual situations, you won't always be toting around everything you've brought with you. In the next few pages, items in bold are things you may want to keep aside for your day pack—the small rucksack or fanny pack for holding items you want to keep handiest on the trail.

Personal Stuff/Toiletries

❏ **sunglasses and/or prescription glasses in hard case**
❏ toothpaste
❏ toothbrush
❏ dental floss
❏ **lip balm with sunscreen**
❏ **sunscreen**
❏ moisturizer
❏ **insect repellent**
❏ **personal medications and prescriptions**
❏ comb/brush, hair accessories
❏ biodegradable soap and shampoo
❏ towel, baby wipes
❏ **toilet paper, mini tissue pack**
❏ **bandanna**
❏ clothes (see page 22)
❏ _____
❏ _____
❏ _____

Use travel-size containers that can be refilled each time you go camping. Products such as combination shampoo/shower gel, and moisturizing sunscreen with insect repellent, can also save money and space.

Equipment

❏ **your copy of *Hit the Trail!***
❏ **field guides**
❏ **maps and compass** (see page 73)
❏ **pocketknife** (see page 21)
❏ **notebook and pen**

- ❏ **whistle with neck cord**
- ❏ **mini flashlight**
- ❏ lantern, candles
- ❏ **extra plastic bags** (resealable and large garbage sizes for dirty clothes, litter, and experiments) (see page 45)
- ❏ **water bottle**
- ❏ walking stick (see page 49)
- ❏ day pack or fanny pack
- ❏ _____
- ❏ _____
- ❏ _____
- ❏ _____

Sleeping Gear

- ❏ sleeping bag in stuff sack
- ❏ sleeping pad or air mattress
- ❏ tent, fly (outmost protective layer of tent), and accessories (stakes, line, mallet)
- ❏ _____
- ❏ _____
- ❏ _____
- ❏ _____

Kitchen Gear

- ❏ cooler
- ❏ mug
- ❏ spoon, fork, and knife
- ❏ bowl/plate
- ❏ spatula
- ❏ pan
- ❏ aluminum foil
- ❏ empty coffee can (see pages 37 and 89)
- ❏ premade trail snacks (see page 40)
- ❏ food (see pages 35–39 for some recommended edibles)
- ❏ oven mitt/cloth
- ❏ _____
- ❏ _____
- ❏ _____
- ❏ _____

Special Items

❑ extra tarp (sturdy waterproof canvas or plastic sheet) (see pages 26, 27, and 46)
❑ plaster of paris for making mold of tracks (see page 54)
❑ fishing rod and tackle
❑ red cellophane (see page 87)
❑ looseleaf and construction paper (see pages 91–93)
❑ paper glue (stick)
❑ **camera and film**
❑ **binoculars** (see page 59)
❑ magnifying glass
❑ playing cards, travel games
❑ empty plastic juice jug (see page 46)
❑ _____
❑ _____
❑ _____
❑ _____
❑ _____

The Just-in-Case Kit

❑ **list of people and telephone numbers to contact in an emergency**
❑ **two or three dollars in change**
❑ nail scissors
❑ several feet of strong rope and twine; bungee cords
❑ duct tape
❑ needle and strong thread
❑ extra batteries and bulbs for flashlight, lantern, camera, etc.
❑ a few paper clips
❑ small tube of superglue
❑ **butane lighter or waterproof matches in a waterproof container**
❑ extra pair of glasses
❑ safety pins
❑ **water purifying tablets or drops** (see page 44)
❑ **first-aid kit with manual** (see page 20)
❑ _____
❑ _____
❑ _____

First Aid

● ● ● ● ● ● ● ● ● ● ● ● ● ● ● ● ● ● ● ●

Accidents happen. Careful planning and preparation, along with a little common sense, can prevent most accidents, but sooner or later one will happen. Remember that the most important thing you can bring is your own knowledge and awareness. Most accidents happen when you're in a hurry, so slow down, be careful, and pay attention to your surroundings. Avoid trouble before it happens, and stay calm if it does. Make sure you bone up on the survival tips on page 78 so you'll be prepared, just in case you ever find yourself in a jam.

A first-aid kit is one of the most important items in your bag. Your first-aid kit should be big enough to suit the size of your group and your method of camping. If you're car camping, your first-aid kit can be bigger than if you're backpacking. Start with a store-bought kit, and add any special items you'll need for where you'll be camping, or any special needs of someone you're camping with. Here are the things all first-aid kits should have:

Your Emergency Kit

● ●

❏ small first-aid booklet (these are usually supplied with a first-aid kit and are very helpful)
❏ adhesive bandages (assorted sizes and shapes, including butterfly bandages)
❏ gauze pads (assorted sizes)
❏ adhesive tape (one small roll)
❏ antibacterial cream

❏ cortisone ointment
❏ elastic bandage
❏ small scissors
❏ tweezers
❏ safety pins
❏ antacid
❏ diarrhea medicine
❏ talcum powder
❏ moleskin or blister pads
❏ instant cold pack
❏ hydrogen peroxide or alcohol pads
❏ small mirror (for checking injuries and for signaling)
❏ pain reliever
❏ calamine lotion (or other cream for itches or stings)

Sharp Knife Tips

● Always, and we mean always, cut away from yourself, not toward yourself! If the blade should slip, it will not cut you.

● A sharp knife is a safe knife; keep it sharp. You don't need to press hard with a sharp knife when you cut, so you are less likely to slip and cut something you didn't want to cut, like your finger. Be sure to buy a whetstone when you get your first camping knife. Sharpening a knife with a whetstone is easy; just follow the instructions that come with the stone.

● Don't throw your knife (that's dangerous!) or stick it in the ground. This will dull—or even break—the blade.

● Use the right-size blade for the job. For example, a big old bowie knife is great for cleaning your toenails if you're Paul Bunyan, but the main blade on a penknife will be far more useful for cutting rope or sharpening a stick. Big knives are hard to control and heavy to carry around.

● Keep your knife clean and dry. After you use your knife, wipe it off with a cloth. Be sure to start wiping with the dull side of the knife, not sharp edge first! Also, rub a drop or two of lubricating oil over the blade with a cloth every once in a while to protect it against rust.

Dressing for Success

● ● ● ● ● ● ● ● ● ● ● ● ● ● ● ● ● ● ● ●

In the great outdoors, best-dressed means you're breezy in the summer, toasty in the winter, and prepared for any weather in between (that means dressing in layers). Here's what you'll want to wear to stay hot (or cool) on the trail.

Tip: Footwear should be sturdy, supportive, lightweight, and comfortable. If there's room, bring a spare comfy pair. If you need new walking shoes or hiking boots, buy them a few weeks before the big trip. This will give you plenty of time to break them in, and not the other way around!

Warm-Weather Wear

● ●

Rain-Forest Rhonda

- hat or cap
- sunglasses
- cotton T-shirt
- long-sleeved shirt
- sweatshirt/sweater
- whistle
- shorts
- thin socks, thick socks
- shoes or boots
- bandanna
- sunscreen
- bug repellent

Cool-Weather Wear

Tundra Tommy

- wooly hat
- sunglasses
- long johns
- turtleneck
- sweater
- whistle
- warm coat
- gloves or mittens
- scarf
- warm pants
- boots
- sunscreen

Bandanna Bonanza

The paisley patterns used on bandannas originated in India. This square of many uses was made popular by the British who settled in the United States. Back then, instead of red, most bandannas were blue, brown, gray, or black, since durable red dye wasn't available until the 1800s. Here are just some of the many uses for this necessary accessory: napkin; headband; washcloth; nose and mouth cover for protection from dust or cold; extra sunshield worn underneath your hat; flag or signal for help; pot holder; bandage for first-aid emergencies; trail marker; theatrical prop for scary ghost stories; ruler—one side of a standard bandanna measures 22 inches, and its diagonal is 31 inches.

Setting Up

You've carefully planned, packed, and prepared for your adventure. Now you're finally here. The next thing you have to do is figure out where you should set up camp.

Campsite Ahoy

● ●

Follow these campsite guidelines and you'll experience smooth sailing in your home away from home.

Water: To avoid being flooded out or polluting water, never camp closer than 100 feet from any waterway. Latrines should be at least 100 feet away from the water and downstream from camp. Don't put your food along the same trail as your latrine. You wouldn't want to run into a bear on a midnight run to the bathroom! (See page 41 to bear-proof your food.)

Wind: Check the wind direction, and remember that breezes flow downhill at night. Hang food 30 yards downwind of camp. Your tent door should face downwind. There should be trees for shade and shelter from wind, but not directly over your tent or fire. The fire ring should be 15 feet downwind from the tent. Firewood (if allowed) should be protected by trees or a tarp.

Surface: It's hard to stake your tent on rocky or sandy ground. Even if your tent doesn't use stakes, you'll get a better night's rest on smooth, even ground. Avoid pitching your tent across a slope, but if you have to, keep your head uphill. Take a look around for ant colonies or hornets' nests so you won't have to move your site once it's all set up.

Impact: Try to make as few permanent changes to your surroundings as possible. One of the best places to set up camp is where someone else already has camped. Chances are it's a good spot, and the area has already been affected.

A "site" for sore eyes . . . or sore backs, feet, or whatever. This campsite is a perfectly planned place—a paradise for any outdoor enthusiast.

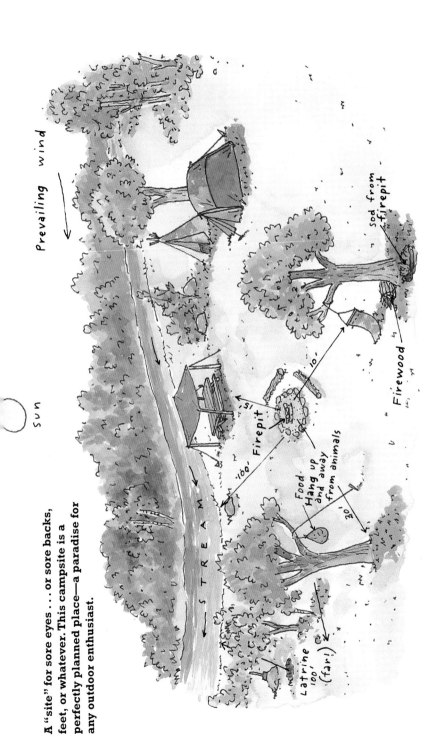

Tent Commandments

● ●

Your home on the range may range from one that pops open to one that requires tools to set up. But no matter what kind of tent you have, the better care you take with it, the better care it can take of you. Keep these rules in mind to make pitching a tent easier:

1. Lay out all the parts and make sure everything is there *before* you go on your camping trip. Toss in extra tent stakes— like socks, they're always getting lost.

2. Practice setting up and taking down your tent at home. Don't be forced to rely on instructions in the dark or in the rain!

3. Use a ground cloth; that's a sheet of plastic that goes underneath your tent. It should be the same size as the bottom of the tent. If it's bigger, any water that lands on the ground cloth will flow under your tent and soak through your tent floor.

4. Use a floor cloth. It isn't essential, but this sheet of plastic or mat you put on the inside floor of your tent can prevent damage to the bottom of your tent. For further protection, always take your footwear off before entering your tent. Place them some- place dry, but handy, such as between the inner walls and fly (the outermost layer) of your tent or in a plastic bag in your tent.

5. Pack a hammer or mallet for pounding down stakes.

6. Keep the stake lines tight and check them often, especially if you've already had to tighten them. (When a tent gets wet, it stretches out, but when it dries, it shrinks.)

7. Always follow any written instructions that came with your tent for putting it away. If you fold it into the same sharp creases over and over, you may weaken the coating and the fabric.

Gimme Shelter!

● ● ● ● ● ● ● ● ● ● ● ● ● ● ● ● ● ●

R eady to graduate to building your own abode? Try this tepee on for size. It's a modern replica of the ones used by the Native Americans of the Great Plains. Sleep in it, play in it, or just build one for the fun of it.

You'll need: 12' x 9' plastic tarp, 15 feet of cord, 8 to 10 wooden chopsticks or shish kebob stakes, 8 to 10 wooden poles about 7'6" to 8' long and 1½" to 2" thick, scissors, a marker, a tape measure, a knife, a small saw (an awl would be helpful).

1. Cut the tarp. Fold the plastic tarp in half so it forms a rectangle, 6' by 9'. The fold you just made is the center line of the tarp. Use a marker attached to a line or string to measure and mark the radius as shown. Cut the tarp to the pattern shown. Don't forget to poke the small hole toward the top. Save the leftover pieces from the tarp to use as a ground cloth or to make a camp chair (see page 46).

2. Tie the tarp to the poles. Thread a one-foot piece of rope through the hole in the tarp. Take one of the poles and position it so that it almost reaches the bottom edge of the tarp. Tie the pole in place.

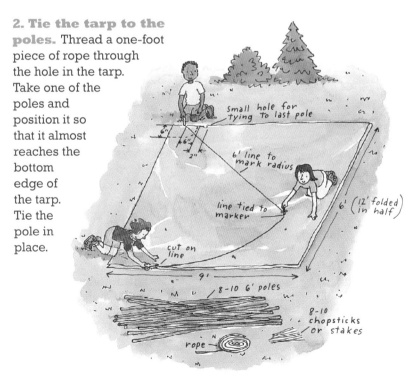

small hole for tying to last pole

6' line to mark radius

line tied to marker

6' (12' folded in half)

cut on line

9'

8–10 6' poles

8–10 chopsticks or stakes

rope

Start and finish with clove hitch

3. Make the frame. Next cut a piece of rope about five feet long. Use this rope to loosely tie three poles together about one foot from the top using a half hitch (see page 30). The poles should stay together at the top, but you should be able to spread them out at the bottom. Now pick a spot for your tepee. Stand the poles up and spread them out to form a tripod. Lean the rest of the poles against the tripod, filling in the empty spaces.

Add additional poles by leaning against first three.

4. Choose the doorway. Decide where you want the entrance of your tepee. Then lift the pole tied to the tarp on the side opposite to where you want the entrance. The entrance should be on the downwind side.

5. Cover the frame. Wrap the tarp around the frame of poles. The bottom edge should reach the ground all the way around, and the ends of the tarp should overlap by four to six inches. If the ends don't overlap at the top, take the whole tepee apart and tie the three poles together a little lower down. If the ends do not overlap, or if the bottom edge does not reach the ground, just move the bottoms of the poles closer together.

6. Pin the tarp together. With help from a grown-up, use a knife to sharpen one end of each wooden chopstick. Starting at the top of the tepee, overlap the ends of the tarp so it is wrapped tightly against the poles. Poke the chopsticks through both ends of the tarp to pin the tarp together. Work your way down the opening of your tepee, putting the chopsticks in about 12 inches apart. Leave an opening big enough for you to crawl in and out.

Chopsticks 12" apart

holes for chopsticks when flap is closed.

7. Finish the tepee. Tighten the tarp by working around the outside, moving the bottoms of the poles out. Then tuck the bottom edge of the tarp under the poles. You can also use large rocks inside your tepee to hold down the bottom edges.

Tepee Etiquette

In your home, you probably have to wipe your feet before coming in. Well, in the 1800s, some Native Americans were following these rules in their homes:

● If the tepee door was open, a visitor could walk in.

● If the door was closed, the visitor was to announce his or her presence and wait to be invited in.

● Men sat cross-legged. Women sat with their legs to the side.

● Men entered a tepee and went to their right. When women entered they went to their left.

● A younger person did not speak until an older person spoke to him or her.

Knotting to It

● ● ● ● ● ● ● ● ● ● ● ● ● ● ● ● ● ● ●

Need to whip up some nifty camp gear or make a swift repair? Knot a problem! This selection of powerful knots will save the day.

Clove Hitch: Since this knot needs tension to hold tight, it's a perfect knot to use to lash poles together with a rope. A clove hitch lets the rope be tightened or loosened. You would need to use this type of knot to make something like the tepee on pages 27.

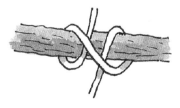

Two Half Hitches: Two are better than one when you want to attach a rope to a pole or an object. Unlike the clove hitch, this knot ties something off more securely. Use two half hitches to bear-proof your food. (See page 41.)

Taut Line Hitch: This is used for tying off a rope to an anchor point. Just slide the knot up to tighten the rope. Use a taut line hitch to tie tent lines to pegs.

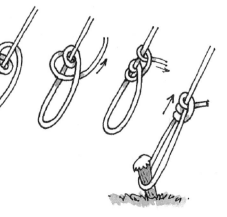

Square Knot: You don't have to travel to the four corners of the globe to tie this knot! One of the most common knots around, this one is for tying together the ends of two ropes of equal size. You would use a square knot to tie a bandanna around your head or neck, or to fasten together the two ends of a neck cord to keep your binoculars handy.

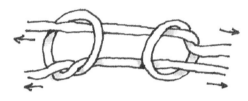

Fisherman's Knot: There's nothing fishy about this knot—it's used to join two pieces of thin rope to make one longer rope that forms a perfectly straight line when taut. The fisherman's knot is ideal to use if you have two pieces of rope—one three feet long and the other seven feet long—and wanted to make a ten-foot rope.

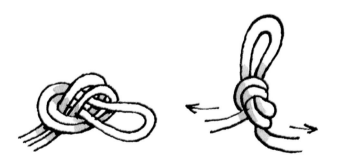

Loop Knot: This knot is used to form a loop in some rope so that you can attach something to it, like a lantern. If you make a loop knot on the end of a rope, you can use it to hang gear from pegs, hooks, or branches.

Make Yourself at Home

Ah! You've found your camp, set up and explored the area, and you're probably as hungry as a bear. Now's your chance to build a campfire! Sure, fire can be fun, but only if it's handled safely. Make sure you answer these burning questions (and get the okay from a grown-up) before you get going on your gourmet grilling. As with any part of camping—but especially fire—the idea is to leave as little impact on your campsite as possible. If you have your heart set on a huge bonfire, remember: Small fires do less damage than big fires.

Starting Fires

Am I allowed to build a campfire here?

Find out if campfires are allowed in the area, and if they are allowed only in the firepits or grills provided. Is wood gathering forbidden? Is firewood available at the ranger's office, or at the nearest store? Before starting a fire, you must know and obey the area rules on campfires and fuel.

How do I find and prepare a safe site for the fire?

If the campsite has an existing grill or firepit, always use that one. If you're starting from scratch, try to find an area that has gravel, sand, or loose soil to keep the scar your fire will leave behind to a minimum. Otherwise, dig a pit about twelve inches around and eight inches deep. Fold back or carefully remove the grass layer, which is called sod. After you are through with the firepit, you can extinguish the fire (see page 34), and replace the sod.

Clear the area of flammable material for six feet in all directions. There should be no overhanging trees.

What kind of fuel will I need to start and keep my fire going?

You'll need three basic types of fuel for your fire:

• **Tinder** is the easily ignited material that first gets the fire going. Good tinder options are dried leaves, grass, bark, or tiny sticks. In a pinch, newspaper or cotton wool can do the job.

• **Kindling** is a little bigger and thicker than tinder and will catch fire from the tinder. Look for sticks and twigs from a quarter to half an inch thick.

• **Large branches or logs** are the last things to catch fire. You'll use the coals and flames from this main fuel to cook, sing, toast marshmallows, and tell ghost stories by.

Never break wood off trees—not even dead trees. Cut wood only in an emergency.

What kind of fire do I need?

Different fires produce different types of heat. All require a clear area and rocks to prevent the fire from spreading. Here are four common types of fires and their best uses:

• **Tepee fire:** Make a tepee shape with pieces of wood. Light the fire from below. This fire will burn hot. The embers are good for frying foods.

Caution: Do not rest pots and pans directly on a tepee fire—it isn't strong enough to support the weight. Instead, use the keyhole technique below.

• **Keyhole Fire:** Using large dry rocks, make a shape that roughly looks like a keyhole. Build a tepee fire in the circular section. Scrape the coals into the lower portion of the keyhole, and use this lower part of the keyhole to cook your food.

● **Trench fire:** Dig a trench following the direction of the wind. The trench should be sloped with the shallow part on the end the wind blows into. Line the sides with rocks to further insulate the fire, to retain heat, and to keep the walls from falling in. This type of fire is best used where there is a danger of starting a forest fire during a drought, in heavy winds, or where there are a lot of dry leaves.

● **Star fire:** Put logs in the shape of a star, with their ends almost meeting in the middle. Start the fire at the center where the logs meet. Keep moving the logs closer to the middle of the fire as they burn. This is a good small fire to heat a single pot on. Just balance the pot on top of the logs in the center.

How do I start the fire?

Very carefully! Start with a small amount of tinder. Build a little tepee, or stack some of your smallest kindling on top of this. Fire needs plenty of air, so make sure not to put in too much kindling at first. Keep some kindling aside to add later. Place the flame at the very bottom of the tinder. Make sure your kindling fire is really going before you add bigger pieces of fuel. If your fire starts failing, start to feed it the kindling you've kept aside.

The Human Fire Extinguisher

T he most important part of using a campfire is knowing how to put it out properly.

1. Sprinkle water all over the campfire pit.

2. Carefully sprinkle water onto the embers; then stir them with a stick to moisten them thoroughly.

3. Repeat this until you no longer hear any sizzling or feel any heat rising from the embers. Have a grown-up double-check that the fire is completely out.

Cool Tools and Great Grub

N ow that you know how to start and keep a safe fire, it's about time for a good hot meal. Here are a few simple recipes and easy-to-make tools you can use, to turn your weenie roast into a fiery feast. The best thing about these meals is that there's little or no clean-up!

Forked Fry-Up

Instead of packing a heavy frying pan, whip up this lightweight substitute—it's a natural for grilling burgers.

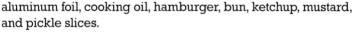

You'll need: a forked stick with a handle that's at least ½ inch thick and at least two feet long, aluminum foil, cooking oil, hamburger, bun, ketchup, mustard, and pickle slices.

Wrap the forked part of a stick in aluminum foil to make a small frying pan. Put a very small amount of oil in the center of the aluminum foil. Place a hamburger patty in the center of the pan. Watch the meat sizzle and cook. Remove the pan from the fire, and use a fork to flip the burger. Continue to cook the hamburger until you see no pink meat when you cut it in the center. Toast your bun or bread on your frying pan. Add mustard, ketchup, and pickles to taste.

Egg in a Basket

Use your forked frying pan to make this delicious dish any time of the day.

You'll need: bread, a cup, oil or butter, an egg, salt, and pepper.

Place a piece of bread on a firm flat surface. Use the open end of a cup as a cookie cutter to cut a circle out of the center of the bread by twisting it against the bread. Put the cut-out circle back in the hole. Put some butter or oil on your frying pan or forked fryer (see page 35), and place the bread on it. Place the frying pan over the fire to lightly toast the bread. Remove the pan from the fire, and place it on a flat surface. Remove the cut-out bread circle and put it aside. Flip the bread, and crack an egg over the hole. Hold the frying pan back over the fire until the egg is cooked. Remove the pan from the fire, slide the food onto a plate, sprinkle on salt and pepper to taste, and eat up!

Come-and-Get-It Kebabs

You can cook just about anything on a straight sharpened stick. Green wood from a freshly fallen tree makes the best sticks, since it won't burn. But if there is no fallen green wood available, soak dry sticks in water for a few hours before you need to get cooking.

You'll need: a sharp knife, sticks; one-inch slices of hot dogs, sausage, beef, chicken, or fish; cherry tomatoes, onion wedges, mushrooms (eat only store-bought mushrooms, since it's hard to identify edible mushrooms in the wild), pineapple chunks, zucchini, potatoes cut in half-inch cubes, or peppers (bacon slices can be wrapped around just about everything); a forked stick; and pita bread.

Spear your chosen ingredients onto a stick that's whittled down to about 15 inches long and half as wide as a pencil. Brush the kebabs with some cooking oil, and cook over your fire, turning as each side browns. You may have to cut into the meat chunks to find out if they are thoroughly cooked. Thread the prongs of a forked stick through a pita so that it lies flat. Toast the bread over the fire. Take the pita off the stick, wrap it around your kabob, and pull all the ingredients off the stick. Eat from the pita.

Stone Griddle Quesadillas

If you're ready for some fancy fireworks, try a little Mexican food on for size.

You'll need: a large dry flat stone about eight inches long, six inches wide, and 1½ inches thick, cooking oil, soft tortillas or pita bread, spatula, shredded cheese, salsa, diced tomatoes, and shredded lettuce.

Wash the stone. Wipe it dry. Allow it to dry completely. Place it in the hot coals for at least 15 minutes. Using an oven mitt (and with the help of a grown-up), pull the rock out to the edge of the fire. Lay a sheet of aluminum foil on it, and toast both sides of a tortilla or pita. Add some shredded cheese, and allow it to melt. Carefully remove the soft tortilla or pita from the stone with a spatula. Allow to cool slightly. Add salsa and tomato and lettuce. Roll up the tortilla or pita, and dig in. If the stone starts to cool off, place it back in the hot coals for at least 10 minutes. Then start again.

Caution: Don't ever put wet stones in a fire, because they might explode—it's extremely dangerous!

Popcorn Can Can

It doesn't take much to make some buttery munchies over an open fire.

You'll need: a coffee can, a wire hanger, oil, popcorn, aluminum foil, oven mitt or cloth, butter, and salt.

With the help of a grown-up, use a can opener to carefully punch two holes on opposite sides of the opened end of the coffee can we told you to pack. Insert the hanger through the holes, and twist-close to form a secure handle. Pour enough oil to cover the bottom of the can (about one tablespoon). Then put in three tablespoons of popcorn. Wrap aluminum foil loosely over the top of the can. Poke a small hole in the center of the aluminum foil. Using an oven mitt or cloth, hold the can over the fire, and wait for several kernels to pop. Shake the can until you don't hear any more corn kernels popping. Add butter and salt to taste. Let the can cool before digging in. (Don't try this with a regular tin can—the edges are way too sharp, and you can easily cut yourself!)

S'more than Dessert

Your campfire meal isn't really over until you've had dessert! Try one of these fireside treats to satisfy your sweet tooth.

Build a Banana Boat

Even if your camp is nowhere near a body of water, you can still enjoy this boat. And when you're done carving one out for yourself, you'll probably want to build a boatyard-full for your friends! Who wouldn't want to make some more—some more Banana Boat s'mores, that is!

You'll need: a banana, a knife, chocolate chips, mini marshmallows, forked frying pan, aluminum foil, graham crackers.

1. Peel back, but don't peel off, the top strip of the banana skin. Without cutting through to the other side of the banana, cut the banana in half the long way. (You may need help from a grown-up.) This is your boat.

2. Put chocolate chips and marshmallows into the banana. Fold the skin of the banana back over the entire delicious dinghy. Wrap aluminum foil around the entire banana, making sure the banana is completely covered.

3. Now it's time to cook your creation. Place the boat on the grill or coals, or your forked fryer (see page 35). Prop it up with a wedge of aluminum foil so it doesn't

capsize. Your Banana Boat needs to cook only until the marshmallows and chocolate melt, which is about ten minutes in a fire.

4. Take the wrap off carefully. You wouldn't want to waste any of your precious cargo! Peel back the banana skin, and slip your boat onto a graham cracker. Separate the two banana halves and cover the sticky ship with another graham cracker. Go ahead, take a bite! Now we can't think of a better recipe for a happy camper, canoe?

Leaf It to Chocolate

Make chocolate-covered mint leaves to decorate desserts, or just eat them by themselves.

You'll need: mint leaves, paper towels, chocolate chips, a small pot or aluminum foil, forked frying pan, and a knife.

1. Wash and dry mint leaves thoroughly.

2. Put the chocolate chips in a small pot over a fire. You can make a pot out of aluminum foil and place it over the fire on your forked fryer (see page 35). Stir occasionally to keep the chips from burning. When the chocolate has melted, stir it one final time to smooth out any lumps.

3. Take the container off the fire. Dip your knife into the chocolate sauce, and spread a thin layer of chocolate on top of the mint leaf.

4. Place each leaf on a dish and put the dish in a cool place (like the cooler!) for at least 15 minutes.

Tip: Strawberries dipped in chocolate are a "berry" tasty dessert, too!

Trail Treats

● ●

Here are a few recipes for snacks that are healthy, lightweight, nonperishable, and delicious! Just put them in sturdy, resealable bags, pop in your daypack and you're ready to go.

GORP
● ●

The name stands for Good Ol' Raisins and Peanuts, but GORP can include just about anything.

You'll need: peanuts, raisins, popcorn, chocolate chips, dried fruit, sunflower seeds, nuts, crunchy wheat or corn cereal, granola, mini pretzels, or mini marshmallows.

Choose ingredients from this list, add some of your own favorite munchies, and pour them together in bag.

Rib Stickers
● ●

These sticks were made for walking—go for a dip when your stomach starts to grumble.

You'll need: celery, carrots, apples, bread, peanut butter.

Cut the fruit, vegetables, and bread into sticks. Put peanut butter in a small container with a lid.

Fruit Leathers
● ●

Here's another tasty snack for the trail.

You'll need: 2 cups of strawberries or blueberries, a potato masher, a bowl, a cookie sheet, some sugar, waxed paper.

Mash the berries. Spread the mixture onto a cookie sheet and sprinkle with some sugar. Let the mixture dry. (It may take several days.) When the fruit leather is dry, lay a sheet of waxed paper over the top. Roll the leather up like a jelly roll. Cut the larger roll into one-inch rolls.

Don't Feed the Animals

While you're camping, it might seem mean not to share and share alike, but when it comes to feeding your furry and feathered friends, here are three reasons why it's better to keep your servings to yourself:

• To reserve your food supply. Chances are there will not be a grocery store near your campsite.

• For your safety. Although it may seem fun to feed small animals such as squirrels or raccoons, they may carry diseases like rabies that cause serious illnesses in humans.

• For the animals' sake. If an animal loses its fear of humans, it can become a pest or a danger. If it is then removed from the campsite, the animal will probably be destroyed rather than returned to the wild. Don't be the cause of senseless killing.

Un-Bearable Food

Plastic bags won't be enough to protect your food in bear country. To keep your food bear-proof, it's best to hang it from a tree, since bears not only can bite through plastic, they can bite through a cooler!

You'll need: a rope at least 30 feet long, a strong waterproof sack, and of course a tall tree with a long branch at least ten feet out from the trunk. Tie one end of the rope to the food-filled sack with two half hitches. Hoist the bag up until it's hanging three feet below the branch. Tie the other end to the tree trunk with a clove hitch. Your food and you are now pretty safe from any hungry bears. (See page 30 to find out how to tie these knots.)

Plants and Flowers

I f you want to add a spontaneous salad to your meal, here's a beautiful bouquet of flowers and plants that look good enough to eat. And you can! This is a list of a few widely available edible flowers and plants. Remember: Only pick plants if it's allowed, and then only if you're 1000 (yes, 1000) percent sure you know what they are!

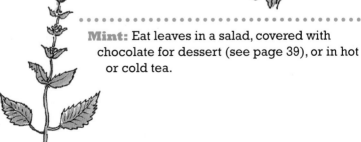

Lunch is ready!

Daisy: Young leaves can be eaten raw in a salad. Flowers can be dried to make tea.

Dandelion: Root can be boiled in salt water and eaten. Stems, leaves, flowers, and buds can be eaten as a salad or cooked in butter with bacon in a frying pan.

Mint: Eat leaves in a salad, covered with chocolate for dessert (see page 39), or in hot or cold tea.

Rose: Flowers are eaten raw after bitter white base has been removed. Tea can be made from flowers, leaves, or rose hips (the flower after maturing).

Wild Strawberry: Berries can be eaten raw, or cooked. Stems and stalks can be eaten in a salad. Dry older leaves for tea. (See page 39 for a "berry" delicious dessert.)

Wild Onions: Fresh onions can be put on insect bites and boils. Eat raw or cooked.

Tip: While you're hiking or setting up camp, look at the beautiful plants around you. A good plant and flower field guide is a valuable tool for learning about and identifying plants.

Painful Plants

Here are a few plants that you definitely shouldn't put in your salad, or anywhere else near you! Learn to identify these important plants and you'll be able to avoid some very uncomfortable situations!

Poison Ivy

Poison Oak

Poison Sumac

Water Works

● ● ● ● ● ● ● ● ● ● ● ● ● ● ● ● ● ● ● ●

No matter whether you're rafting to an unexplored part of the Brazilian rain forest, trekking to the top of Mount Everest, or camel riding through the Sahara Desert, don't drink the water! Water from even the most remote areas carry tiny organisms, diseases from animals, and chemicals from humans that can make you very sick. The only way to make sure that you have safe drinking water is to use water sources that are identified as safe, or to bring your own. If you're in a situation where you have to drink from a natural source, there are several methods you can use to treat the water.

You can try to kill the bacteria in the water by boiling it for at least fifteen minutes, but that's no guarantee of safe drinking water, and takes a lot of fuel and time.

There are chemicals that come in drops or tablets that sanitize water, but some make the water taste funny. These are a good backup should something happen to the water you've brought. Follow the instructions, and always check with a grown-up before you use them.

Another way to get clean water is to buy a filter system that pumps water through filters to remove contaminants.

How Much Water Do You Need?

Don't drink water from the outdoors, but do drink at least ten glasses of safe drinking water a day. Your body is 75 percent water. You can go without food for weeks, but your body will suffer without adequate water. It's as important as nutritious food for keeping you safe and well fueled on the trail. If you need to bring water to your camp for drinking and cooking, each camper will require at least three quarts of water per day.

Water in the Bag

It's best to do this early in the day and to remove the bag by midday or before the sun really hits that part of the tree. Put a plastic bag over a branch of a tree. Close off the opening of the bag with a twist-tie. You probably won't get enough water to quench your thirst (besides, we just told you never to drink water from an outdoor source unless it's an emergency!), but it's a cool way to see condensation (the process of water vapor turning into liquid) in action!

Campsite Comfort

● ●

Most people think camping means roughing it, but that's not necessary! After you settle in to camp and fix yourself a tasty meal, it's time to add a little touch of luxury to your home away from home.

Forest Faucet

This easy-to-make device can serve as a sink or as a (very quick) shower. Hey, someone has to do the dishes!

You'll need: a nail, a plastic juice jug with a handle and twist-off cap (the thicker the plastic the better), some round twigs, a knife, two feet of string, some water, and four to five feet of rope.

1. Using a nail, poke a hole about two inches from the bottom of a clean jug. This is the spout.

2. Sharpen one end of the smallest twig. Use it to enlarge the nail hole. If you want a bigger stream of water, just use a thicker twig to poke a larger hole.

3. Tie a string to the twig that fits the hole and attach it to the jug handle to use as a stopper. Fill the jug with water. Tie a rope to the handle, and hang your outdoor faucet up on a tree branch.

Tip: You can control the flow of water by loosening (more water) or tightening (less water) the cap.

Chill-Out Camp Chair

Here's how to make a lightweight, portable chair. It's a lot like a type of chair used by the Native Americans of the Great Plains. If you have already made a tepee out of a tarp, you should have all the materials, tools, and skills to make the chair.

You'll need: a sheet of strong cloth 2½' x 6', or the leftover piece of tarp from the tepee (see page 27); a knife or scissors, a strong straight stick or dowel about 3 feet long with a diameter of about 1½ inches; three wooden chopsticks or metal shish kebab skewers, or three straight strong twigs about 8 inches long; 10 to 12 feet of strong cord or light rope.

1. If you're using the leftover piece of tarp, you can make two chairs. Cut it down the middle, then cut off the semicircles.

2. Fold the cloth over the strong stick with about 6 inches of overlap. Take the chopsticks and pin the material together, just the way you did with the tepee to hold it closed.

3. Cut a length of cord about 7 feet long. Tie the ends of the cord to the ends of the stick, using two half hitches. (See page 30.)

4. Tie the leftover cord to the middle of the other cord, then to an overhead branch. The cross stick should be about three feet above the ground. Instead of using an overhead branch, you can make a tripod like the one for the tepee and hang the chair from that.

5. Now all you need to do is sit down and relax. The chair can be packed into a small bundle; just leave the stick and tripod behind.

Adventures Abound

Walk softly and carry a big stick." Okay, okay, so when President Theodore Roosevelt said that, he wasn't actually talking about hiking. But keeping the words of one of the greatest outdoor enthusiasts in mind—along with a few of our own tips—will help you walk wisely.

Best Boot Forward

● ● ● ● ● ● ● ● ● ● ● ● ● ● ● ● ● ● ●

● Try to stay on the established trail. This way you won't be hurting any habitats, foliage, or beautiful views.

● Wear clothes with colors that blend into your surroundings. The harder it is to see you, the more likely it is that you and others on the trail will get a closer view of wildlife, such as a mother deer and her fawn. The brightly colored bandanna in your day pack can always be brought out if you need to be spotted more easily.

● Try to walk quietly, and don't talk too loudly. The harder it is to hear you, the more likely you and others on the trail will be to see or hear a woodpecker drill for its dinner.

● If you are wearing water-resistant footwear, go through puddles instead of around them on the trail. This will help keep you from widening the path and destroying the surrounding plants.

● Most trails don't provide containers for trash or recyclables— soda cans, toilet paper, or food wrappers. And none of these should be left behind—not even biodegradable food wastes. Garbage attracts animals, who quickly learn that humans have food. This situation could potentially pose a dangerous problem for both humans and animals. Always keep a bag in your day pack to collect everything you need to throw away.

● If you are walking more slowly than other hikers behind you, move over to let them pass. Hiking is not a race for most people. It is perfectly okay to go as quickly or slowly as you want, as long as you aren't interfering in anyone else's hike or losing track of trailmates you're traveling with. Likewise, if you're faster than the rest of your group, for safety's (and good manners') sake, try not to rove too far ahead of your fellow hikers.

Now pack up your daypack and get going!

Stick to the Trail

· ·

A walking stick is a good thing to carry on a hike. The stick can come in handy in a number of ways: to help keep you balanced on steep or uneven terrain, to open the path in front of you when you go through thick brush, or to test the depth of a stream.

A good walking stick should be about the same height as you are, and strong enough not to bend under your weight. It shouldn't be too heavy, because you're going to have to carry it. Some people like to find a new stick for every hike or trip, and others like to keep the same one. If you find one you really like, strip the bark off to expose the smooth wood underneath, at least around the section you use as a handle. A good stick can last for years.

Cloud Clues

● ● ● ● ● ● ● ● ● ● ● ● ● ● ● ● ● ●

While living off the land, you'll need to keep a close eye on the weather. So keep your eyes on the sky. Which direction the winds are blowing from, how high the clouds are in the sky, and how many clouds you see are just a few of the things you need to know to determine what weather is in store. Here are a few important clouds and what they can tell you.

Cirrus: These thin, high, wispy white clouds are also called mares' tails, because they look like horses' tails. They're made of ice particles and usually are a sign that the weather is changing to rain.

Cirrocumulus: These high-altitude, grainy, and layered clouds have the nickname mackerel sky because they look like the stripes on the side of a fish. They typically form as the day progresses and disperse at night. They are usually a sign of fair weather.

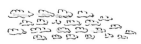

Altocumulus: These middle-altitude clouds look like rows or ripples across the sky. They usually mean that rain is less than a day away.

Stratocumulus: These light-gray thickening clouds are made of water vapor. They are typically found in cold fronts with strong winds. They mean that rain or snow is not far behind. Set up your tent quickly when you see these clouds coming.

Cumulonimbus: Break out the Monopoly game! When you see these clouds, you won't be leaving that tent anytime soon. These are the true rain or snow clouds. They are thick, towering, dark-gray or even black clouds that look like mountains in the sky.

Cumulus: These are the cottony clouds that float by in an otherwise blue sky. These fair-weather clouds usually mean it is a nice day.

Nature's Weather Report

It's hard to beat the TV or radio for a dependable weather report. But while you're out on the trail, there are many methods and old sayings you can use to try to predict the weather. Keep your eyes peeled, and judge their accuracy for yourself.

- "Red sky at night, sailor's delight. Red sky in the morning, sailors take warning." This means that if an eastern sky is red as the sun sets, the front has already passed. If the morning sky in the west is red, then the clouds and rain have yet to come.

- The chirp of a certain cricket found throughout most of North America can tell you what the temperature is. Count the number of chirps you hear for fifteen seconds. Then add 32 to get the Fahrenheit temperature.

- Pinecones close up tightly when it will rain, and open for clear dry days.

- "Short to notice, soon to pass; long to notice, long to last." A fast-moving cold front will bring rain, but it won't last long. The gradual change of a warm front usually brings a longer steady rain.

- Bees stay near their hives if rain is due.

- Spiders spin long webs on hot dry days and no webs when rain is due.

- "Dew in the morning light means no rain before the night." In order for dew to form, the air needs to be cool and clear—not a condition that brings rain.

- A ring around the moon means rain will come.

- Seaweed on the shore is shriveled up for dry days and swollen and damp before it rains.

Animal Hide and Seek

● ● ● ● ● ● ● ● ● ● ● ● ● ● ● ● ● ● ● ●

You've made your weather report and are ready to hit the trail! Seeing wildlife is one of the best things about camping. However, being seen is the last thing most animals want. Use these tips to increase your chances of spotting life in the wild.

● Look for horizontal lines in the woods; this could be the back of a deer.

● Humans evolved as sight predators with excellent vision. Your instincts will help you find things. Scan your view, and check out anything that doesn't look right.

● Pay attention to small patches that are lighter or darker than the surrounding landscape.

● Check the edges of fields and clearings. Most animals don't like to venture too far from the security of cover.

● You don't have to see an animal to know it's been around. They leave all kinds of signs, like: footprints, "scat" (a tracker's word for poop), hair or feathers, or leftovers from a meal. Learning how to find and recognize these signs is a big part of being a good tracker.

● Look for tracks along the water edge where there is soft ground.

● Sunlight and wind make tracks deteriorate, so think about that when you guess how old tracks are.

● If it's very dry, or if there are no good places to find tracks, clear a spot where you think animals will walk such as an intersection of two trails. Wet the ground, and check the spot the next day. Look on page 56 to identify some common mammal tracks.

Animal Sense

Use all your senses to try to find wildlife:

● See if you can find hair caught on a fence. Look for nutshells left by squirrels or clipped plants eaten by deer or rabbits. Search high up in trees to find a squirrel's nest of a clump of leaves or a bird's nest.

● Listen for rustling, screeching, or calling.

● Keep a field log like the Animal Sighting Sheet we've provided on page 55. List the names of the animals you see, how many you see, and any signs that the animals have been there. At the end of each day, check your notes. For those animals you didn't identify, try to use your notes, the critter guides in this book, and any field guides you brought along to solve the mystery. Take note of the sounds you hear, and look through guidebooks to try to identify the animals that make them. (See page 94.)

Be Kind to the Animals

Respect them for safety's sake—yours and theirs. This means: Don't feed them! Animals that are fed by humans lose their fear of us and can become aggressive. If an animal is too much of a nuisance at a campground and has to be removed, it might be killed, not relocated.

If you see a nesting bird, don't go near it. The bird will be forced to get up from its nest. Even if it abandons its spot for only a short time, this disturbance leaves the eggs exposed to other animals and to cooler temperatures.

It's a myth that fallen baby birds are abandoned by their moms. Most birds will feed their young, even on the ground. Try to remember that wild animals are best kept that way—wild, and best left in the wild. Don't "save" an animal by bringing it home.

Don't try to get a closer look at an animal by chasing it. You may chase that animal into a spot where it feels cornered, and then it may attack you.

Animal Tracks

● ● ● ● ● ● ● ● ● ● ● ● ● ● ● ● ● ● ● ●

There's nothing like finding a good animal footprint to reward your keen tracking ability. It doesn't matter if you don't actually see the animal make the print! What's important is that you find the track and recognize that an animal has been nearby. Besides, your buddies at home will be impressed with a footprint of the animal that got away.

You'll need: a paper towel, a paper cup (or paper milk carton), plaster of paris, water, and some newspaper.

1. Make sure there is no water in the track. You may need to gently blot the track with a paper towel to dry a damp or wet imprint.

2. Cut a paper cup in two. In the bottom part of the cup, mix the plaster of paris with some water to make a mixture with the thickness of pancake batter.

3. Now put the upper part of the cup around the track so that the track is in the center of the ring.

4. Gently pour the plaster over the track to fill up the ring.

5. Wait at least an hour for the plaster to harden. Dig up the cast, and wrap it in newspaper.

6. Remove the ring of paper and use water to clean the cast. At home, you can use an old toothbrush to get all the dirt off the cast.

Tip: While you wait for the cast to dry, fill out a copy of the Animal Sighting Sheet on the next page. Even if you saw the track and not the actual animal, you can still figure out a lot! Is the track going toward a stream or away from one? Maybe the animal was on its way home or had just finished drinking water. Make a tracker's guess about who left the track.

Animal Sighting Sheet

Species _____

Sex   ❑ Male   ❑ Female

Age   ❑ Adult   ❑ Immature

Place _____ Date _____ Time _____

County_____ State _____

Behavior ❑ Feeding   ❑ Resting

             ❑ Traveling   ❑ Other _____

Type of Environment

❑ Pine Forest   ❑ Deciduous Forest   ❑ Marine

❑ Open Field   ❑ Town   ❑ Wetland

❑ Lakeside   ❑ Other _____

Weather/Temperature _____

❑ Clear   ❑ Snowing   ❑ Cloudy

❑ Windy   ❑ Raining   ❑ Other

Notes:_____

_____

_____

_____

_____

Sketch:

Mammals

White-Tailed Deer: These browsing animals eat twigs and leaves instead of grass. Whitetails are common in most of North America. They can be found in a large number of habitats but prefer edge cover, which is where different habitats meet. Look for them in open fields early in the morning or in the evening. Take care if you're camping in the spring; fawns are born then, and they will lie still until you almost step on them.

Raccoon: These animals like to live in wooded areas and are mainly nocturnal, which means they're most active at night. Raccoons are omnivorous creatures and will eat just about anything. In the wild, raccoons mainly eat small animals. But these clever creatures are more well known as mischievous members of the Campground Clean Plate Club. Their dexterous hands can also open just about anything—including garbage cans and coolers!

Skunk: These woodland buddies will eat just about anything and prefer to make their rounds by the cover of night. They compete with the raccoons for camp leftovers. There's one main difference: These creatures come with a loaded rear end—their handy defense against enemies. If they have a chance, they try to give a warning, but if you miss the warning, your camping trip will really stink!

Opossum: Like kangaroos and koalas, these animals are marsupials, which means they have pouches—the only ones in the western hemisphere. Opossums can use their long flexible tails to grasp things like branches. They make their dens just about anywhere dry,

and line them with nests of grass and leaves. They eat small animals, fruits, and grains. These natural actors are known for playing dead when they're in danger. Watch for them scurrying across the road at night.

Coyote: These loners are masters of survival. They used to live primarily in the West, but coyotes have made a huge increase in the entire eastern half of the United States. These small, wolflike animals are carnivorous, eating mainly small mammals such as rabbits and mice. Coyotes are very secretive creatures, so they're more likely to be heard than seen. *AHHH-OOOOOO.*

Red Fox: These adaptable animals are closely related to dogs and jackals and live in burrows. Foxes feed mostly on rodents but have been known to eat birds, frogs, and fish. Look for foxes in open fields as they hunt for mice. Not all red foxes are red. They may be black or any mixture in between.

Beaver: These brown furry creatures are the largest rodents in North America. Beavers have webbed back feet and flat hairless tails that look like canoe paddles. Beavers create their own habitat by damming small streams, or they may live in small lakes and rivers. They survive mainly on bark and woody vegetation, but also eat water plants. When they are startled, they make a loud splash with their tail. Look for beaver dams and their domed-shaped homes, or for their gnaw marks on trees near water.

Bigfoot: A BIG hairy thing that lives in the Pacific Northwest. Bigfoot has a cousin called the Yeti living somewhere in Tibet. Bigfoot is generally a shy, peaceful vegetarian, but will occasionally be driven to eat children between the ages of eight and twelve.

The Invisible Camper

● ● ● ● ● ● ● ● ● ● ● ● ● ● ● ●

One of the best ways to catch a glimpse of shy creatures is to make a blind. Most animals are better at spotting you than you are at spotting them; their life depends on it. If you make a blind, they'll have a harder time seeing you, and you'll be able to watch them as they feed and move around. A blind can be as simple as a couple of branches piled around you. It's most important to build your blind in the right place and to sit still and be very quiet. Here are a few other tips:

● Have something large, such as trees or large rocks, at your back. This will hide your outline and give you something comfortable to lean against. Clear the area where your feet will be so you won't make noise.

● Put the blind near where two trails meet or where you've found tracks and other animal signs.

● Place the blind so your scent doesn't blow toward the place you expect the animals to be.

● Use your peripheral (side) vision.

Bird Watching

● ●

Serious bird-watchers keep a life list of all the species of birds they have ever seen. You don't need much equipment to be a bird-watcher, and you can do it the whole time you're camping.

You'll need: a good field guide for birds to help you identify the birds and tell you about them, binoculars, and a small book to keep your life list in. (See page 55, Animal Sighting Sheet.)

Bird-watching is more than just watching. You can also listen. Birds are very vocal. Many sing to attract a mate. Crows scream to warn their friends that danger is approaching. Ducks will call to one another to tell where the food is. Mockingbirds like to imitate the songs of other birds. And, if you are ever in the woods and hear a loud "*KEE KEE KEE*," duck your head and run the other way. That's the sound of a goshawk, warning you to get away from her nest before she decides to dive-bomb you.

A fun thing to do is to track down a singing bird. When you hear a bird calling in the brush, try to find the bird and actually see it calling. While you're trying to find the bird, memorize the song. Later, try to write a description of the song in your bird-watching log. Some people like to make up a saying to help them remember the song. The robin's song has been described as "cheerily cheer up, cheerily cheer up."

Binoculars

Binoculars are a big help when you look for animals. Of course, they help you see things that are far away, but they also help you see in thick woods. By looking through spaces in bushes and trees, you can see what's behind them. Binoculars also help gather light, which comes in handy when you track at dusk and dawn, when animals are most active.

When you hold binoculars, steady them by keeping your elbows at your sides. Sometimes it's hard to locate something in the binoculars' field of view. To solve this problem, look at what you want to see and bring the binoculars up to your eyes without taking your eyes off the object.

Wow, these things look really close!!

Birds

Birds of Prey

Buteo: Includes red-tailed hawk, broad-winged hawk, red-shouldered hawk. These hawks hunt in wide-open spaces and in areas that are both forest and fields. They hunt rodents like rabbits or mice by flying off a perch like a tree limb. Look for their light undersides either when they're soaring high overhead or when they're sitting in a tree or on a telephone pole. Their large nests are easy to spot high up in trees.

Turkey Vulture: These birds eat carrion, which is a nice word for dead animals. They are easy to spot in flight since they look like black flying letter Vs. To be sure you are looking at a vulture, watch for a rocking motion as it sails on the wind. If you see a large black bird with a red head munching on road kill, you can be fairly certain it's a vulture. You may also find them on the ground when they're laying eggs, since they don't build nests in trees, but in rotted tree stumps or logs.

Kestrel: These are the smallest falcons in North America. They are about ten inches long and are a rusty red color. Since they eat mostly insects like grasshoppers and crickets, you can find them hovering over fields. Kestrels lay eggs in hollow trees. The female will refuse to leave her nest even if threatened by another animal like a fox, or you.

Northern Harrier: These rodent-eating hawks hunt over open fields or wetlands. They fly slowly and low to the ground looking for their dinner of mice or little birds. They have long wings and tails. The females are a chocolate brown on top, and the males are a dull gray. For some unknown reason, harriers, like most hawks, don't prey on other birds that nest around them.

Waterbirds

Great Blue Heron: These birds feed on frogs and fish, so you may find them wading along shorelines of lakes or streams. They look like great big storks and really are a grayish blue. They fly with slow wing beats and with their legs extended. They build their nests in large colonies, in trees over either salt or fresh water. You may see the males bringing nest materials and the females building the nests.

Belted Kingfisher: Kingfishers are well named because they are excellent fish catchers. Watch for these blue birds with yellow bills hovering and diving over water. They build burrows in banks above water. Both the males and females help to build burrows in banks above water.

Perching Birds

Red-winged Blackbird: These birds eat insects like mosquitos and also eat seeds from either fields or forests, but they love marshy fields. You can spot the males by the bright red-and-yellow patch on their wings. In the spring, they are usually in meadows singing to attract a mate. When the birds pair up, they build nests in rushes and reeds along the water.

American Goldfinch: It's hard to miss these striking yellow-and-black canaries. They zip around in a roller-coaster flight pattern. Like blackbirds, goldfinches eat seeds and insects. If you find a nest in the fork of a tree that is deeper than it is wide and lined with thistle and cattail down, you've probably found a goldfinch nest.

Streamlife Safari

● ●

If you're aware of what to look for along a stream, you can open up a whole new world of wildlife exploration. If you like slimy rocks and gooey mud, there's no better place to find them than in a stream or creek. You can also find all kinds of little creatures if you know where to look. With the following equipment, take a walk along a brook and see what you find. (See page 79 and 80 for water safety tips.)

Finding and Catching Creek Critters
● ●

You'll need: old sneakers, water shoes, sandals, or rubber boots (Wearing some sort of foot protection is very important. Besides stepping on a sharp rock or broken glass, you might get a toe pinched by a crayfish); a coffee can or large cup, another coffee can or bucket, and butterfly net.

1. One of the best places to find streamside animals is under rocks. Turn rocks over carefully. Remember to lift the rocks slowly; this will help keep the water from getting too muddy. Wait for the water to clear, and see what you've found. Don't forget to look on the underside of the rock, too, because lots of bugs will cling to them. It's important to always put rocks back gently in the position you found them. They are often used by small animals as their homes.

2. As you approach the water, move quietly and always look ahead. Search the edges of the stream for frogs, turtles, and other animals that are hunting along the banks too.

3. If you want to catch any of the things you find, use the coffee can or cup. Slowly put the can where you think the animal will go; then gently direct the critter into the can with your finger or a stick. You also have to be careful of what you're catching— be careful so you don't hurt them and they don't hurt you. If you don't know whether something can hurt you, just leave it alone and put the rock back.

4. When you're exploring in flowing water, try to walk upstream, or against the current. This will ensure that any muddy water you stir up will flow away from you and leave you with a clearer view through the water.

5. If the stream you're exploring has a lot of crayfish, you can save the larger ones in the bucket for a special appetizer before dinner. Just boil them in water for a few minutes until they turn red. Break off the tails, and suck the meat out.

Important: Always make sure there are no restrictions on any animals you may want to capture, even for food.

6. It's tempting to keep the animals you find as pets, but it isn't a good idea. If you keep the creatures you've caught they can run out of oxygen and die. Even if they made it to your home, would you know what to feed them so they wouldn't die? It's really best if you return them to their place in the wild and in the food chain. But before you say good-bye, check them out. Take a picture of them, and with them! And don't forget to write about them on your Animal Sighting Sheets. (See page 55.)

Water Strider

Reptiles and Amphibians

Reptiles are cold-blooded animals with dry scaly skin. "Cold-blooded" means that their bodies do not produce heat as mammals and birds do, but their body temperature varies with their environment. Reptiles lay their eggs on land. Amphibians are also cold-blooded, but they have slimy skin because they have mucous glands. Unlike reptiles, they lay their eggs in the water.

Reptiles

Garter Snake: The most common snakes in North America, they can be found almost anywhere. They are medium-sized green snakes with three yellowish stripes along their bodies.

Common Water Snake: These are usually aggressive snakes that feed heavily on frogs and small fish. They are brownish snakes with bands around their bodies, typically found around water.

Rattlesnake: These are poisonous snakes that locate prey with two heat sensors on their snouts. They give birth to live young, who are born with fangs and poison. Rattlesnakes and other pit vipers have triangular heads and thick, heavy bodies.

Water Moccasin: These fat black snakes are poisonous. The insides of their mouths are so white that they are also called cottonmouths. They live in swamps and rivers in the southeastern United States.

Coral Snake: These yellow-black-and-red banded snakes are related to cobras. Like cobras, they have a very deadly poison. They look a lot like the harmless scarlet king snake. To tell them apart, remember this rhyme: "If the nose is black, stay back!"

Box Turtle: These turtles reportedly can live for more than a hundred years. They are yellow-and-black tortoises with shells that close completely.

Snapping Turtle: This is a mostly plant-eating ancient species whose family has been around for 25 million years. These are big muddy brown turtles with jagged edges along the back edges of their shells. They live in ponds, lakes, and rivers. Snapping turtles are well named, so don't mess with them.

Amphibians

Bull Frog: These frogs can grow to be twelve inches long and will eat anything they can fit in their large mouths (even baby turtles!). Look for bull frogs along the shores of quiet ponds, or listen for their deep croaking at night. Also look for tadpoles in late spring and early summer.

Salamander: Most salamanders hatch from eggs. They have gills and can breathe underwater; then, as adults, they breathe air. Look for them under rocks and debris in wet areas or along streams.

American Toad: Toads live their adult lives on dry land but return to the water in the spring to mate and lay eggs. In the spring, listen and look for toads around ponds at night with a flashlight.

Fishing

● ● ● ● ● ● ● ● ● ● ● ● ● ● ● ● ● ● ● ●

Good anglers understand they're not trying to catch a fish but trying to get the fish to catch them. Reeling in the fish is the easy part (unless the fish is a 500-pound marlin)—the hard part is getting it to eat your bait. Try to catch fish by following these rules:

1. Don't let the fish find out you're there. There are two ways for the fish to know you're there, by seeing you and by hearing you. Fish can only see a certain area above the water surface. Next time you're swimming, go underwater, roll over, and look up. That is the "window" the fish can see out of. To avoid being seen by fish, stay low and wear dull-colored clothing. Fish are very sensitive to sound, which can be heard through the ground, so walk softly.

2. Get the fish to find your bait. This means that you have to find the fish, then get your bait in front of it. Like land animals, most fish like to have some sort of hiding place and food close by. Try fishing around weeds and logs and next to rocks. Remember that in moving water, fish typically stay still and wait for food to come to them. The best way to know where the fish are is to see them. Polarized sunglasses are a big help in seeing fish because they cut the glare and let you see underwater. Most fishing stores sell inexpensive polarized sunglasses (brown is the best color). When you walk along the bank, move quietly and look for a long shadow in the water. If you scare or "spook" a fish, note where it was lying, because there's a good chance it will come back. Try the spot later, being extra careful to stay quiet while you approach the spot.

3. Have your bait look and act naturally. Don't make the fish suspicious. A worm sitting still in the middle of a fast current just doesn't look right. Try to make your bait or lure move like the real thing. A small lure tied to a thick fishing line won't move well.

Tip: Find out what the fish are eating—your bait or a lure should be the same or close to the same thing. It's helpful to catch what the fish are eating in a net to get a better look at it. If the fish are feeding on bugs, try to determine what types of bugs by using the bug guide on page 68. Use copies of the Animal Sighting Sheet on page 55 to record the type of bugs, fish, and wildlife you see.

The following two knots are the only ones you need to know for most fishing situations:

Clinch Knot: Use this knot for tying the line to the hook.

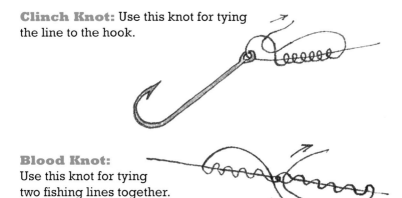

Blood Knot:
Use this knot for tying
two fishing lines together.

Tip: Wet the knot with saliva before you tighten it up.

Something Fishy

Even if you're in an area where they allow you to keep the fish you catch, why not capture them on film instead? By taking a photo instead of a fish, you will give that fish a chance to grow to maturity, and you maybe even get to catch it again.

Here's a little trick used by the the finest anglers around: When having your picture taken with your prize catch, hold the fish away from you and toward the camera. Point the fish head at the camera, and lean back. This is an optical trick that makes the fish look much bigger than it actually is.

side view

Bugs

● ● ● ● ● ● ● ● ● ● ● ● ● ● ● ● ● ● ● ●

Scientists divide the animal kingdom into a series of groups. Starting at the largest, a phylum, it gets more specific with class, order, family, genus, species, and subspecies. The arthropods, which include spiders, insects, and crustaceans, are the largest phylum of animals. There may be as many as two million species of insects alone! Describing even a few of them would be a big job, but this guide can help you identify the class, and maybe the order, of a bug you've found.

1. How may pairs of antennae does it have?
If it has two, with at least five pairs of legs, it's a crustacean. Crustaceans include crayfish, lobsters, crabs, shrimp, and the common little *sowbug.*
If it has one or none, keep answering.

2. How many pairs of legs does it have?
If it has four, it's an *arachnid.* Go to number 3.
If it has three, it's an insect. Go to number 5.
If it has a lot, go to number 4.

3. If it's an arachnid, how many body segments does it have?
If it has one body segment, it could be a mite, a daddy longlegs, or a *tick.* If it has two, it's a spider or a *scorpion.*

4. How many pair of legs per body segment?
If it has two, it's a diplopod. Diplopods are commonly called millipedes. *Millipedes* eat decaying plants and are harmless.
If it has one, it's a chilopod. Chilopods are commonly called *centipedes.* Centipedes are carnivorous, eating small insects. Some of the larger tropical species can be very poisonous.

5. **If it's an insect, it can be one of twenty-eight orders. Of these orders, the most common ones are:**

Coleoptera
Beetles, including ladybugs and fireflies, have hard, glossy front wings and powerful jaws.

Diptera
True flies, midges, *mosquitoes,* horseflies, and tsetse flies feed on plant and animal juices.

Hemiptera
True bugs include bedbugs, *stinkbugs,* and water striders.

Homoptera
Cicadas, grasshoppers, and aphids all feed on plants and can do considerable damage to crops.

Hymenoptera
Bees, wasps, and *ants* are social insects that live together in hives or nests; many have stingers.

Lepidoptera
Almost all *butterflies* and *moths* have four broad, some-times colorful wings. Adults feed on nectar or not at all.

Odonata
Dragonflies and damselflies have long bodies and four narrow, clear wings.

Trees

Trees can be identified by the shape of their leaves, but they also can be identified by their overall shape, or "silhouette." Look over the list of leaves and tree silhouettes below, and keep an eye out for them when you're out in the woods. Conifers or evergreens trees have needles for leaves, which they keep all year. Deciduous or broad-leafed trees lose their leaves every year.

Conifers or Evergreens

Pine: Silhouette—tall shape with horizontal branches. Leaf—long needles in clusters of two to five. Cones are open and very coarse, sometimes with prickles.

Spruce: Silhouette—tall triangular or steeple shape with upcurving branches. Leaf—short four-sided needles, which grow along branches. Cones are tighter than pinecones, with smoother scales.

Fir: Silhouette—triangular shape, upper trunk is not visible through the needles. Leaf—short, flat needles. Cones have tight large scales that stand upright.

Hemlock: Silhouette—irregular triangular shape with a rounder top. Leaf—short flat needles similar to fir needles, but on small stalks. Cones are small and tight.

Cedar: Silhouette—conical shape with a short stem. Leaf—scaly or sharp needles. Produces a small bell-shaped cone and dark berries.

Deciduous or Broad-Leafed Trees

Shagbark Hickory: Silhouette—tall, oblong shape with many branches. Leaf—typically five leaves per stem. A well-named tree with outer bark sticking out. The nut is surrounded by four thick pieces of shell.

Sugar Maple: Silhouette—symmetrical oval tree with branches that point upward. Leaf—green on both sides with three major points with small points on scallops. Sugar maple seeds, called keys, form two "helicopter" blades.

White Oak: Silhouette—broad expansive shape with gnarled branches. Leaf—seven evenly lobed leaves without points. Oak trees produce acorns, which are an important food for deer and turkeys.

Sycamore: Silhouette—very large, irregularly shaped tree. Leaf—has five major points with small points on scallops. The brown flaky bark lets the white underbark show.

Tulip: Silhouette—one of the tallest deciduous trees; branches typically angle upward. Leaf—four points, with smooth rounded edges. Tulip tree flowers look like large white tulips.

Weeping Willow: Silhouette—large round tree with drooping branches that hang. Leaf—small, long, thin, and pointed with small points on edges. This tree is native to Asia.

Tip: If you take a look through a tree identification book, it won't take long to notice that someone had a great time naming trees. Try to find at least two types of trees with funny names. Write them down and make a sketch of their leaves in your journal. (See page 91.)

Food Chain Reaction

● ●

You've had a chance to see, or at least read about, a lot of different kinds of animals and plants. If you've noticed how these living things fit together and depend on each other for survival, then you've had a glimpse of the food chain. The food chain is a complicated relationship between the sun, Earth, and all living things. The earth provides water and carbon dioxide. The sun provides energy from its light and heat. It's pretty amazing, but all the living things on this planet are linked together in some way, forming a huge, complex chain.

At one end of the chain are the plants. They support the animals along the rest of the chain. The plant kingdom, which ranges from microscopic plants to the giant redwood trees, makes up 87 percent of all living things.

Next on the chain are the plant-eating animals. This includes single-celled animals, worms, butterflies, mice, deer, and elephants. They're the most common type of animal, and make up 10 percent of the world's living things.

The last part of the chain, and just 3 percent of life on Earth, are the carnivores—that includes you. (Okay, even if you're a vegetarian, you're able to eat meat, so you're still at this end of the chain.) Being on this end may seem like a good thing, but we also are more dependent on the rest of the chain for support.

When something goes wrong along the food chain, the rest of the food chain suffers.

All animals rely on plants to make the food they eat and oxygen they breathe. In return, animals produce the carbon dioxide that the plants need, they spread seeds around, feed the soil, and when they die return minerals to the earth.

That's how the food chain works. Here is how it looks in the wild: Look around you. Can you find at least three examples of the food chain in action? If you're eating lunch as you read this part of the book, follow what you have in your hand to the source of its existence. (Now we've even given you a head start!)

Using a Map and Compass

● ●

Now you know where you stand on the food chain. But do you know where you want to go and how to get there? Orienteering is the use of a map and a compass to find your way from place to place. It's gone from a necessary tool for survival to a growing sport. Orienteering is easy and can be a lot of fun. But most important, knowing how to do it may save you from spending a cold night lost in the woods.

Polar Bearings
● ●

Earth has two north poles. It could get kind of confusing, but the reason for the two poles can be explained this way: Maps are made pointing toward the geometric center of the earth, which is called the "true" north pole. Compass needles point to the magnetic center, which is called the "magnetic" north pole. The difference between true north and magnetic north is called declination. Any map used for orienteering will tell you the declination of your location by giving you the direction and number of degrees magnetic north is off from true north. It's not a big deal, really; you'll learn how to adjust your compass on the next page.

The Map

. . . .

A topographic map or topo map has wavy contour lines, which show you the lay of the land. When you see contour lines—also called elevation lines—that are very close together, that means the land is very steep. When you see contour lines farther apart, that means the land is flattening out.

A quick explanation of scale: One inch = 1,000 feet means that one inch on the map equals 1,000 feet in the real world. A map with a scale of 1:24,000 means every one length of anything on the map is equal to 24,000 of them in the real world, whether it's one inch or one pinky-finger length.

Tip: The U.S. government has made detailed maps of the whole country. These maps are very helpful at showing you what's around your camping area. You can find them at camping stores, or you can call 1-800-USA-MAPS.

The Compass

. . . .

Here's an orienteering compass. Take a good look at it to get familiar with the names of all of its parts.

Notice that the compass dial is marked with the 360 degrees that make up a circle. North is always at 360, east at 90, south at 180, and west at 270. Any direction can be described by its degree and a compass will tell where it is.

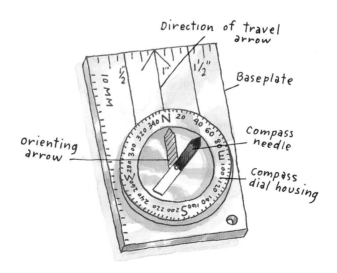

Orienteering Made Easy—The Basics

You'll need: a topographic map and an orienteering compass.

Step 1. Orient your map:

A. Line up the N on the dial with the arrow on the base plate.

B. Next you have to adjust your compass for magnetic north (declination). To do this, turn the compass dial the extra degrees left or right that the map says is the declination.

C. Spread out your map and place the long edge of your compass along the north/south edge of the map.

D. Now rotate the map and compass until the compass needle points to the N. Your map is now pointing to true north.

Step 2. On your map, find your present location and locate where you want to go:

A. Put a bottom corner of the compass base plate on the map where you are located. Keep it there.

B. Rotate the base plate around until the long edge of the compass base plate points to where you want to go.

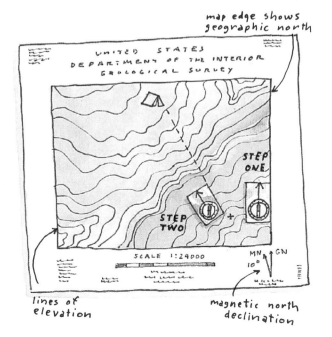

C. Now spin the dial until the N and orienteering arrow are pointing in the same direction as the compass needle. The direction of travel arrow and degree number are now lined up in the direction of your destination.

Note: The number at the direction of travel arrow is your degree reading. If you get lost or you want to show off, you could say "Don't worry, as long as we keep a bearing of [number of degrees], we'll be there by sunset.")

Step 3. Find the way to go:

A. Now, stand up and hold the compass in front of you.

B. Turn your body around until the needle points to the N on the dial again. The direction of travel arrow will be pointing at your destination even if you can't see it.

C. Go that-a-way! To stay on course, look in that direction and find a landmark like a tall tree in line with the direction of travel arrow.

Steps 4, 5, 6.... On the way to your destination:

Walk to the landmark you sighted. Keep sighting and walking to specific landmarks until you reach your destination. Congratulations, Sacajawea would be proud! (She was the Shoshoni guide who helped the Lewis and Clark expedition explore the Pacific Northwest.)

Orienteering Made Easy—The Extras

Locating Using Logic: The shortest distance between two points on a map is a straight line. But in the real world of mountains, swamps, rivers, and roads, the shortest line might not be the easiest or fastest way. The trick is to pick the best route. Look at your map carefully, and try to "see" what the contours/elevation lines are telling you. Where can you cross a river? Is there a trail or road that will get you close to your destination? Break your trip up into little sections, or legs, and use the compass to get you from point to point.

Stepping on the Scale: Use the scale of the map to figure out how long it will take to get from place to place. If the average person walks about three miles an hour and your destination is one mile away, how long will it take you to get there? (Oh no! A word problem!) It should take you about twenty minutes. So, if you haven't found it in half an hour, you might have missed it.

Taking Careful Measures: Measure the total distance of your trip with a piece of paper. Place the corner of the page at your starting point, then line up the edge of the paper with the end point of the first leg of your trip and mark the paper. Now rotate the paper around that first destination point until the edge of the paper lines up with the end point of the next leg of your trip. Mark it and repeat until you've reached your final destination. Measure the distance on the paper against the scale of the map. You can check several routes to see which is the shortest. Factor in any obstacles such as finding a place to cross a stream, or climbing steep hills. Look for the best route to take.

Double Features: If you get lost, look on your map for at least two landmarks, like mountain peaks or lakes. You'll need two points you can see from where you're standing. If you can't see two features, you may have to move to a place where you can. Sight your compass at one of the mountain peaks, and turn the dial until north and the needle line up. Now put an upper corner of the base plate on the mountain peak on the map. Rotate the base plate around the mountain peak until the needle lines up with north again. Draw a line along the edge. Repeat this on another mountain peak. Where the two lines cross is your location. If you can find a third point, this will make sure you're right where you think you are.

Avoiding and Escaping Natural Dangers

● ●

While exploring the outdoors, getting lost may be the most common problem you'll have. (Check out page 73 to learn how to use a map and compass.) But just in case you find yourself in less likely, but very dangerous situations like forest fires or rock falls, or face to face with a bear, here are practical ways to get yourself out of trouble and back into fun.

Forest Fire Facts

Because forest fires are rare, many people don't know what to do once one occurs.

Do Not

● Climb a canyon wall or steep slope, as these make great chimneys.

● Wet your clothes since water will heat up and scald your skin.

● Take deep breaths in a smoky area. Instead, breathe through a piece of cloth.

● Hide in a cave or enclosed area, since the fire could surround you and use up all the oxygen.

Do

● Stay calm.

● Leave the area as soon as you think there is a fire, no matter how far away the fire may be.

● Travel downhill, since fire travels four or five times faster uphill than down.

● Stay in lower-lying areas, or in a pond or stream.

Lightning Storms

- During a lightning storm, make sure that you are not at or near the highest point around.

- If you are swimming, get out of the water. Water conducts electricity.

- Stay away from anything metal, including your backpack if it has a metal frame.

- If you are on a mountain, look for either a shallow cave without an overhang, or a deep cave. It's best to crouch down where it is dry and to avoid touching the walls.

Rock Falls

When hiking on or near a mountain, be aware and careful of rock falls. Rock climbers, great changes in temperature, heavy rains, and animals are the leading causes of rock falls. If the rocks you're walking on begin to slide and you can't avoid the fall, lean into the slope.

Steep Escape

If you get caught on a steep mountain face, practice balanced climbing.

- Your weight should be centered over your feet.

- Let your feet and legs carry your weight.

- You should always have three points of contact with the mountain (either your two hands and one foot, or two feet and one hand).

- Put as much of your shoe as possible in contact with the ledge or other area you're standing on.

- It's important to think about and plan your steps at least two or three moves ahead.

Water Hazards

● If you're going to be around water, learn to swim, or take something with you that will help you stay afloat.

● If you're going out on a boat, always wear a life vest. They look funny, but they may save your life.

● If you fall into a fast-flowing river, position yourself facing downstream with your feet out in front of you. Use your feet to bounce off rocks. Don't try to swim back to where you fell in. Go with the flow.

● Never go swimming alone.

Wild Animal Alert

In addition to staying away from the animals we've already warned you about, remember these tips:

● If you run into a bear or a mountain lion (or an escaped Siberian tiger for that matter), don't run! Instead, back up slowly until you're out of sight, then run like the wind! If you run immediately after seeing them, you might trigger the predators' natural instinct to chase.

● Most of the smaller dangerous animals like poisonous snakes or insects don't want to hurt you. They attack because they feel threatened. Give an animal space and an escape route, and it will usually take it. If it doesn't run away, you should.

● While touching a toad won't really give you warts, most reptiles and amphibians do carry bacteria. Always wash your hands after touching any animal.

Now that you've made sure you can find your way around—and get home safe and sound—make your way back to camp for some dusky delights.

Night Stalkings

Just because the sun has gone down doesn't mean the fun is over! With the first bright sign of fireflies bobbing around the campsite, night mysteries and mischief in the wild have just begun.

For those of you who have never slept outdoors before, or set out for nocturnal adventures, you're in for a great awakening! Nighttime on the trail means an out-of-this-world light show, awesome animal spotting opportunities, and a whole other way of sensing the world around you!

The Stars

● ● ● ● ● ● ● ● ● ● ● ● ● ● ● ● ● ● ● ●

As you sit around the campfire, listen and watch for what the night has to show you. The naked eye can see about 2,000 stars. With strong binoculars, you can see another 200,000 stars!

When you begin your stargazing, start with the most helpful and, luckily, the easiest constellation to find—the Big Dipper. (Check out the star map on page 82 if you don't know what the Big Dipper looks like.) The two stars that make up the outside edge of the Dipper's bowl are called the pointers. By following the line of these two stars out of the bowl, you will find the North Star. If you put your hand up so it looks as if it's in front of the stars, it's about three hand widths from the pointers.

The North Star's other name is Polaris, because it sits above the north pole. Even though Earth's spinning causes the other stars to appear to move, Polaris always appears in the same place at all times. When you find the North Star, you've found north. The North Star is the first star in the handle of the Little Dipper (see page 81).

The San, as the Bushmen of Africa's Kalahari Desert call themselves, believe the stars to be great hunters who chase wild game across the sky. The San even claim to hear stars call out as they track down their quarry. Like the San, the ancient Greeks saw groups of stars as people and animals in the sky. You can still look up and see the same groups of stars, which are called constellations. The Greeks thought one of these constellations looked like a little bear and named it Ursa Minor, which means "little bear" in ancient Greek. Today we call Ursa Minor the Little Bear, or the Little Dipper. A cluster of stars that the Greeks thought looked like a big bear was called Ursa Major, which means "big bear" in ancient Greek. Today Ursa Major is known as the Big Bear, or Big Dipper. Many of the Greeks' constellations can still be seen today. Use the star map to find these and other star clusters.

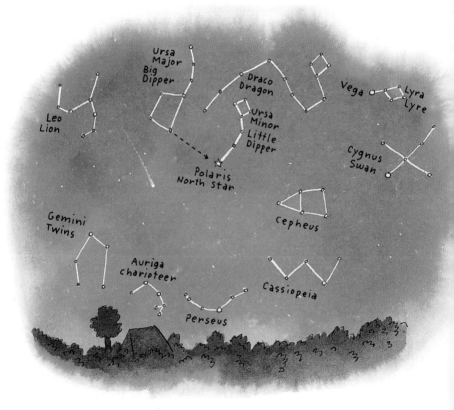

The Planets

● ●

To help figure out if what you're looking at is a planet or a star, remember that stars twinkle but planets don't. The light you see from planets is reflected from the sun.

Out of the nine planets in our solar system, six can be seen without a telescope. One can not only be seen, but felt—it's the planet Earth! The other five planets are Mercury, Venus, Mars, Jupiter, and Saturn. The three planets that cannot be seen without a telescope because they are too far away are: Uranus, Neptune, and Pluto. Since planets revolve around the sun, they move about the sky differently than stars do. The word "planet" means "wanderer" in ancient Greek, and the planets got their name because the Greeks thought they wandered across the sky among the stars.

The planet Venus is silvery. It is one of the easiest to see, since it is brighter than any other planet or star. It is also known as the morning and evening star, because that's when it can be seen.

Mercury is also only visible in the morning or evening but is much harder to see. Both Mercury's and Venus's orbits are inside of Earth's—that is, closer to the sun—so they can never appear very far from the sun, which is why they are only seen in the morning or evening. Look for them in the direction of the rising or setting sun.

Mars is easy to recognize because of its red color, but it's not as easy to find. Since its orbit is outside of ours, it can be seen in the sky at any time. Due to the shape of the solar system, planets can never be seen in the northern sky. Also, during the summer planets will appear low in the southern sky.

Jupiter and Saturn can be seen, but since they aren't as colorful as Mars they're harder to recognize.

Test Your Eyesight

● ●

Look at the brightest star in the handle of the Big Dipper. How many stars can you see? If you see two stars, according to the San, you have very good eyesight. They check their children's eyesight by having them look at the star and asking them to say if they can see the two stars.

The Moon

● ● ● ● ● ● ● ● ● ● ● ● ● ● ● ● ● ● ●

Like the planets, the moon reflects sunlight, which is why we can see it. The moon and the sun appear to be the same size even though the sun is 400 times larger. This makes solar eclipses possible. A solar eclipse happens when the moon comes between Earth and the sun. The moon spins at just the right speed as it orbits Earth, so the same side is always facing us. That's why nobody, except astronauts, has seen the dark side of the moon.

The moon goes through phases:

● It starts with the new moon. The moon is between Earth and the sun, and it cannot be seen.

● As the orbit of the moon brings it around Earth, it will start to show its edge. This is a crescent moon.

● As the moon begins to show itself, it is called a waxing moon. A waxing moon is lit up on the right side.

● Half of the circle can be seen during the first-quarter moon.

● A quarter moon is 90° from the sun. It rises at midnight and sets at noon.

● The full moon occurs when the moon is opposite the sun. It will rise at sunset and set at sunrise.

● The moon wanes as it continues to move around Earth. The last-quarter moon rises at noon and sets at midnight.

● A gibbous moon is between a quarter and full.

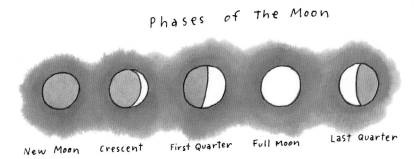

Phases of The Moon

New Moon   Crescent   First Quarter   Full Moon   Last Quarter

Moonwalk

● ● ● ● ● ● ● ● ● ● ● ● ● ● ● ● ● ● ● ●

Take a hike using moonlight to guide the way. First, a word of caution: While very few animals out there in the night would hurt you, there are nighttime dangers. They're not just in the deep dark woods—they're very close by, at your campsite. If you decide to go moonwalking, always make sure you've gotten the okay from, or are with, a grown-up.

When you walk in the woods at night, be careful not to trip over something or to get poked in the eye by things up high, like tree branches. If you have to go by some branches, put your arm up, duck your head, and squint your eyes.

At night it's easy to get lost, so only wander around where you've been during the day. Even though there's really nothing to be afraid of, it's hard not to be at least a little nervous on an after-dark walk.

Nighttime Animal Viewing

● ●

You will need: a regular flashlight, a red flashlight (see page 87), and your walking stick (for feeling your way around and holding up to protect your face from branches).

1. Wear drab clothing. The animals out at night have good vision, so it helps to be camouflaged. Long sleeves and pants will help protect you from any branches or thorns you may bump into.

2. Try to move as quietly as possible. Those nocturnal animals don't have big ears for nothing!

3. Try not to turn on your flashlight. It takes a full forty-five minutes for your eyes to adjust fully to the dark. When our eyes are at their best, humans can see better than bears but not quite as well as cats.

4. Stick to the shadows if it's a moonlit night.

5. Many campgrounds will have a bright light around the bathrooms. These attract lots of bugs, which can attract bats. Try throwing little pebbles up in the air in front of bats; sometimes they will think it's a bug. Watch how they use the webbing between their legs and tail to catch the "bug."

6. Try fishing at night. The biggest fish in the lake like to feed at night. Again, don't turn the light on unless you have to. If you do, turn your back to the water. (Never go near a body of water at night alone!)

7. Try sitting in a blind (see page 58).

8. Pause to look and listen a lot. Use your ears to "see" in the dark. Listen for coyotes howling to one another (they don't really howl at the moon). Listen for the peeps of spring peepers, which are tiny tree frogs, the high thrill of the American toad, or the deep *"broommpp"* of the bullfrog.

Tip: Sounds count too! You don't actually have to see an animal to record it on the Animal Sighting Sheets in your journal. So don't forget to list animals you've identified by sound as well (see page 55).

Nighttime "EYE" D

Nocturnal animals' eyes don't really glow; they are just reflecting the light back. Different animals' eyes reflect different colors, and this can be used to "eye"dentify them.

- **Raccoon** . . . . **gold**
- **Opossum** . . . . **orange**
- **Skunk** . . . . **amber**
- **Porcupine** . . . . **red**
- **Black bear** . . . . **orange**
- **Red fox** . . . . **green**
- **Coyote** . . . . **greenish gold**
- **Bobcat** . . . . **goldish white**
- **House cat** . . . . **green**
- **Deer** . . . . **goldish white**
- **Cottontail rabbit** . . . . **red**
- **Bullfrog** . . . . **green**
- **Alligator** . . . . **bright red**

Seeing Red

Since many animals can't see red light, a red flashlight is an excellent tool for spotting them. It's very easy to turn an ordinary flashlight into a red one.

You'll need: red cellophane, a flashlight, and a rubber band (depending on flashlight).

1. Cut a piece of red cellophane large enough to cover the end of the flashlight. Hold it in place with a rubber band. Trim off extra cellophane so you won't crinkle as you walk.

2. For flashlights that twist off at the end, you can follow the instructions above or try the following. Twist the cap off your flashlight. Cut a piece of cellophane into a circle that fits the inside of the lens. Place the cellophane between the lens and the reflector, and reassemble the flashlight.

Who's Who?

These owls can be found throughout North America. Try to find them, or better yet, call them to you.

● Barred Owls have a call that sounds like someone saying "Who cooks for you? Who cooks for y'all?"

● Great Horned Owls have a low double hoot that sounds like a far-off train.

● Barn Owls have a long piercing scream.

● Screech Owls have a long wail like a ghost.

Campfire Ghouls

● ● ● ● ● ● ● ● ● ● ● ● ● ● ● ● ● ● ● ●

Memorize this scary story to frighten your family. You may want to practice telling it a couple of times before you perform it for others. But be careful! You may scare yourself!

A girl in my school says her family always comes to this camp-ground. Her grandfather told her that when he was a young boy, a family with a young girl often visited the same camp-ground. The girl's family loved to tell ghost stories. One night, while her father was telling an especially scary one, the girl became so frightened she ran screaming into the woods. Her parents called for her to return. They shouted her name, "Lillith!" and waited for her to come back. But she didn't. So they set out to look for her.

With their lanterns, they followed the path they thought she had taken. Into the dark woods they called her name, "Lillith!" They came upon another family out camping. The family had seen Lillith, but when they called to her, she ran away.

Lillith's family searched for hours, but they still did not find her. For the next week, Lillith's family, the police, forest rangers, and people from town looked for poor little Lillith. A lot of campers said they had seen her. They said that while they sat around the campfire telling spooky stories, a girl appeared. But each time someone called to the girl, she would run away.

After months of searching, Lillith's family had to give up. She was never seen or heard from again. That is, she was never seen or heard from *alive*. Some people say she is still around. [Start to talk more softly here.] They say she comes to campsites where there are families, looking for her own family.

Supposedly, [more softly] she wanders the woods looking for campfires. She listens for scary stories being told. [more softly] She follows the voice, only to find that it isn't her family. [more softly]

My friend from school says she saw Lillith coming toward her from the woods. [Now when you get to this point, jump up and look horrified. Point to an imaginary spot over a family member's shoulder and scream] AND THERE SHE IS NOW!!!

[At this point, run away from your audience. See who in your family you scared the most. Chances are he/she will be the one following the closest behind you . . . or is it Lillith?]

Tip: Just as they do at the movies, provide popcorn to munch on during your show. (See page 37 to make your own popcorn tin.)

Special Spooky Effects

- Hold the flashlight underneath your chin with the light pointing up, to give your face an eerie glow.

- When you are about to get to a particularly scary part, lower your voice. That way, your audience will be listening intently and be more startled when you scream or shout.

- Add different characters' voices to your tale to really dramatize the story.

- Use props for special effects. For example: throw paper poppers, pop a blown-up paper bag, and wear a bandanna as a disguise.

- Roll dried beans or small rocks around in a coffee can or cup for a rain sound effect.

- Pour water from a pitcher into a bucket for a running water sound effect.

- Crinkle cellophane or plastic wrap for a crackling fire sound effect.

- Slap two pieces of wood together for a gunshot sound effect.

- Pound your fist into a pillow for a running heavy footsteps or falling thud sound effect.

Homeward Bound

Leaving a campsite is in some ways harder than packing to go and setting up camp. First, there's none of the anticipation of the big trip, just the thought of the long drive home. Second, everything is now a little dirty and maybe a little wet, mixed up into unorganized piles, and somehow, two or three times bigger than you remembered it. Just as before going camping, it's wise to plan and prepare for the journey home.

Packing Up

● ●

Here are some tips to make the tail end of the trip a little easier. Cheer up; as soon as you get home you can put some finishing touches on your journal (see page 91) and use the lists of books and other resources on page 94 to start planning for the next time you hit the trail!

1. Start early.

2. Start airing out your sleeping bag when you get out of it on the morning of your departure.

3. Reorganize your things so they're in the order they were before you left home.

4. If your tent is the free-standing kind, tip it on its side to let the bottom dry off.

5. Count your tent stakes. Do you remember how many you started with? Are you leaving with the same amount?

6. Spread leaves, rocks, and sticks back over your tent site so it'll blend back into the surroundings.

7. Put out your fire, and check to be sure it's out. Then check it again in a little while to be sure it's really out!

8. If you were camping in a wilderness area, replace the sod over your firepit, and disperse the stones and firewood. If you're leaving a campground, pile any leftover wood neatly.

9. Collect all the garbage around the site. If it's worth packing in, it's worth packing out.

10. Do a final check for forgotten items and one last look around. If you've been camping in a wilderness area, besides the matted-down grass, can you tell anyone has camped there? Or is the campsite as nice as, or nicer than how you found it?

11. Keep in mind a saying many outdoor groups have adopted: Take only pictures, and leave only footprints.

12. When you get home, take the time to completely clean off and dry out your sleeping bag, tent, and all your other equipment.

Lasting Impressions

Y ou may have traveled two thousand miles over unknown mountains and prairies, or a hundred yards into the creek in your backyard, but you had a once-in-a-lifetime experience. Record it. Then you can look back for lists of things you wish you'd brought. Read it to see how much you've changed. Refer to it to see where you've been and to help you plan where you're going.

Journey Journal

Why not make a scrap-book of your time on the trail? By adding loose-leaf paper, construction paper, folders, and maps to an ordinary binder, you can make a complete and completely original

scrapbook of this journey. Also, with a big enough binder, you can keep adding pages with mementos from journeys yet to come.

1. Make journal entries.
Use the loose-leaf paper to record your thoughts about the trip. Write down what happened during the day, like:
Who you were with,
What you saw, heard, smelled,
Where you went,
When you went there, and
How far you went.

2. Create a photo album.
Take photographs and list the area and date the pictures were taken. When the pictures are developed, tape them to construction paper you've poked holes in to put next to your journal entries in the binder.
Try making a collage using different photos and mementos to show you having fun.

3. Keep a sketch pad.
Many times, photos don't capture the true essence of a moment. Sketch the landscape, plants, and animals you encountered to keep a more personal record of your experience.

4. Write a story.
It can be fact or fiction. You can add experiences you wished had happened, or leave out parts you could have done without. Maybe you left your new rain poncho behind—or maybe Bigfoot borrowed it!

5. Keep a folder of articles or letters you write about the trip.
If something extraordinary happened to you—a new awareness, a special sighting, a feat you've never before done, write it down. Call your local newspaper, or write a letter to the campground or park ranger sharing your experience with others.

6. Make a map of your campsite.
Draw a map detailing hikes, particular plants or animals, and natural features you can remember. If you go back to that area, you can compare how things have changed.

7. Create your own reference section.
Collect observations you've made of the trip.

● Make rubbings of barks of trees, interesting stone surfaces, or the textures of different plant leaves. It's easy to do; just tape or tie a piece of sturdy paper over the object. Rub crayon or chalk lightly over the object until a pattern emerges. Fix the image with hair-spray or fixative (available at art stores) when you get home. Take note of the location. See if you can find that spot again.

● Put all your Animal Sighting Sheets in one section; be sure to keep adding sheets with each new animal sighting. If you couldn't identify the animal you saw while you were in camp, try to find it in an animal guidebook.

● Make a flower press. Don't destroy any landscape for the sake of your journal, but if picking is allowed in the area you're visiting, you may want to pick a leaf or flower to preserve in your notebook. You may need some glue to keep your pressed plant in place. It would be a good idea to lay a piece of waxed paper over the plant to keep the moisture and pollen and even glue from gumming up the page before it. It would be fun to look up and actually learn the name of the plant from a good plant guide. Write it down on the page next to the pressed foliage.

8. Keep a "Wish I Were There" folder.
This folder could hold brochures, travel articles, or a list you've written describing places you'd like to go one day.

Resources

● ●

Nonfiction Books: Field Guides and Reference

The Audubon Society Field Guide to North America (Alfred A. Knopf, New York, latest editions). Subjects include birds, fishes, whales, dolphins, insects, spiders, mammals, reptiles, amphibians, trees, and wildflowers.

Golden Guides (Golden Press, New York, latest editions) cover a wide variety of topics including: bird life, geology, insects, mammals, seashores, the night sky, trees, venomous animals, weather, and weeds.

Petersen Flash Guides (Houghton Mifflin Co., New York). These guides fold up into a neat card-sized poster with information on topics such as hawks, animal tracks, wildflowers, and birds.

The Wild Wild Cookbook: A Guide for Young Wild-Food Foragers. Jean Craighead George. (Crowell, New York, 1982).

Stalking the Wild Asparagus; the Field Guide Edition. Euell Gibbons. (David McKay Company, Inc., New York, 1962).

Constellations for Every Kid. Janice Van Cleave. (John Wiley and Sons, New York, 1997).

Whitney's Star Finder. Charles A. Whitney. (Alfred A. Knopf; New York, 1985). This book is packed with interesting information and comes with a star-finding disc that really works.

Knowing the Outdoors in the Dark. Vinson Brown. (Collier Books, New York, 1972).

175 Amazing Nature Experiments. Rosie Harlow and Gareth Morgan. (Random House, New York, 1991).

The Kids' Nature Book: 365 Indoor/Outdoor Activities and Experiments. Susan Mildford. (Williamson Press, Charlotte, VT, 1996).

Fiction Books: Good Reading for the Trail

My Side of the Mountain. Jean Craighead George. (Puffin Books, New York, 1991).

Island of the Blue Dolphins. Scott O'Dell. (Bantam Doubleday Books for Young Readers, New York, 1960).

Hatchet. Gary Paulsen. (Simon and Schuster, New York, 1987).

Adventures of Huckleberry Finn. Mark Twain. (Penguin Group, New York, 1983).

Swallow and Amazons. Arthur Ransome. (David R. Godine, Boston, MA, 1985).

Magazines

National Geographic World, magazine for kids 8 years old and up, National Geographic Society, 17th and M Streets NW, Washington, DC 20036.

Ranger Rick, magazine for kids 6–12, National Wildlife Federation, 1400 16th Street, Washington, DC 20036-2266.

Rodale's Guide to Family Camping, (800) 480-1110, and *Backpacker* magazine, (800) 666-3434; both published by Rodale Press, Inc., 33 E. Minor Street, Emmaus, PA.

Equipment

For a look at some cool camping gear, write or call:

Cabela's Camping Catalog, RKD-TDY, Sidney, NE 69160, (800) 800-8706

Campmor, PO Box 700-BA96, Saddle River, NJ 07458-0700, (800)230-2151

L.L.Bean, Casco Street, Freeport, ME 04033, (800)681-2326

CD-Roms and Web Sites

If you have a computer available, you may want to look for:

Exploring North America's National Parks. This program has a directory of the national parks. Find out what each park has to offer to create a travel plan.(Multicom Publishing Inc., 110 Olive Way; Suite 1250, Seattle WA 98101)

Sim Park. Make a simulated living park using over 100 plants and animals in their ecosystems. Learn about each of the plants and the food chain that is ever-changing with each living thing you add to your nature park. (Maxis, Inc., 2121 N. Californian Boulevard, Suite 600; Walnut Creek, NE 94596-3572)

If you have access to the Internet, check out the thousands of Web sites about camping and the outdoors. Since the Web sites change so often, the best way for you to begin your search is by looking up the key words *kids* and *outdoors*. You could also look up GORP, NWF, national parks, camping, backpacking, tracking, and different names of animals, to list a few key words.

Organizations

Many great organizations are dedicated to helping keep the outdoors a wild and wonderful place. Some have magazines that you can subscribe to or borrow from your local library. Others have outings or organized activities designed specifically for kids. You may want to write to them to get more information.

Girl Scouts of the USA
830 3rd Avenue
New York, NY 10022

Boy Scouts of America
1325 Walnut Street
Irving, TX 75038-3096

Sierra Club
730 Polk Street
San Francisco, CA 94109

The Nature Conservancy
1815 North Lynn Street
Arlington, VA 22209

World Wildlife Fund–US
1250 24th Street NW
Washington, DC 20037

We hope we've given you some good information, tips, and activities to use on your camping adventure. We've shared what we've learned with you; would you share your experiences with us? Which activities did you like best? Which information and tips did you use most often? Were you able to spot some animals? We'd like to know. If you found a tip that didn't work for you, or came up with one you think we should have had in the book, write to us at our e-mail address:
Durkin@highlands.com.

S0-CKP-887

LIVE THE
Smart
Way

Gluten-Free &
Wheat-Free Cookbook

Over **90** simply
delicious recipes from
the Smart Kitchen

by
Kathy
Smart

SECOND EDITION 2012

Kathy Smart, Ottawa, Canada

Published in 2012 by
Kathy Smart · Ottawa
www.livethesmartway.com

Food Styling:	Trevor Smith, Bronwyn Lefebvre, Darlene C
Food Photography:	James Park and Answermen Ltd.
Editor:	Sandra MacInnis
Design and Art Direction:	Answermen Ltd.
Editorial Assistants:	Chef Katie Richards, Sabha Jaleel, Linda Houle Roberts, Kathy Smart, Brad Smart, Ryan Latreille and Susan Latreille, Darlene C, Lisa Cantkier, Sabha Jaleel, Adrian Delorey, Blue and Sailor

Copyright © 2012 Kathy Smart
www.livethesmartway.com

Recipe Photos :

Copyright © 2012 Answermen Ltd.
answermen.com

Copyright © 2012 James Park
www.jamesparkphotography.com

Cover Photo of Kathy:
Copyright © 2012 Al Simard

All rights reserved. No part of this book may be reproduced in any form without written permission from Kathy Smart.

Printed and bound in Canada.

A Note from the Author

I have had multiple food allergies from the time I was 4 years old. Eating was more about 'what could I eat?' as opposed to what tasted good. I wanted to change that.

As I grew older I discovered that there were many people just like me with multiple food allergies and limited choices when it came to food. I decided to make a difference, to become part of the solution. I became a nutritionist so I could help others experience the improved quality of life that comes from eating foods that are good for you. Then I became a certified holistic chef so that I could create recipes with those wholesome foods that also TASTED GOOD!

Food is now all about tasting good. It isn't just about whether I can eat it or not; now, its the best of both worlds. Please love and savour every bite—not only can you eat these recipes—they taste good and are good for you!

From my kitchen to yours, join me—Live The Smart Way!

*Photo Credit: Jean Marc Carisse

A Note from the Editor

Food. Sharing it is the one thing that is common across all cultures.

We use it to celebrate the milestones of our lives, to give us sustenance and comfort, to energize and revitalize us each day. In its simplest form, it is fuel, but shared with friends it is the vehicle through which those friendships grow, around the supper table food is a tool through which we love our family and finally it is the parenthesis around which we begin and end each day.

The love of food is a love of life and it is a passion I am grateful to share with my wonderful friend Kathy. I have always been an advocate of the healing qualities of good food, but through our friendship have learned to appreciate that food can be both good and good for you without sacrificing taste and texture. Kathy's gentle-fierce nature has also taught me that you can change your life if you change the way you live, and so now I live a little Smarter.

This cookbook is full of recipes through which you too can love your family and friends, providing them with sustenance for both body and soul, and helping them to live a little Smarter too.

Sandra MacInnis has spent most of her adult life working in the hospitality sector, and her experience runs the gamut from fast food to fine dining. A 12 year progressive career path with Le Cordon Bleu developed her love for food into a passionate belief that the dinner table is central to everything truly important in the world. Sandra currently works as a Foodservice Consultant for Designed Food Systems Inc. in Ottawa, Canada.

Dedication

"All that I am, or hope to be, I owe to my angel mother."

Abraham Lincoln

I dedicate this cookbook to my mother. Words could never describe how much this woman has done to make this world a better place. She taught me gentleness, kindness, and above all else to love unconditionally and without judgement. I dedicate this book to her as it was she who first taught me to cook, who never tired of finding answers to my health problems, and who cooked to find recipes that I could eat.

Kathy learning to cook
- 3 years of age

"Always add love to whatever you are cooking, honey," was her gentle advice.

I always do, Mom. I love you!

Acknowledgements

I didn't even know where to start for this acknowledgment page. I feel like I am at the Academy Awards! I would like to thank the heavens above for giving me a dream at a young age to make a difference in people's health. For my family—Mom, Dad, and Steven and the girls—for always knowing and telling me I was a miracle and I would achieve great things. For my grandmamma for teaching me how to cook pancakes before I could even speak full sentences. For my Uncle Larry who was a chef for 25 years who showed me that food could be beautiful! For Dr. Don Warren for seeing the potential in a little girl at 12 years of age and teaching her she could be whole again with proper nutrition. For Jennifer Steers for asking me 5 years ago if I ever thought of writing a cookbook. For my best friend Kelly who has been loving me and eating my food since we were 4! For my best friend and first client ever, Anne and her husband Alec, and Camille and Marie for not only giving me the best, honest food advice, but for also being the kindest, most wonderful friends ever. For Sandra MacInnis, for being such an instrumental part of this book, and the food world—staying up late editing, cooking and being my yoga girl. To Chef Katie Richard for editing on her weekends off, for Sabha whose constant support and friendship means so much. Thank you to Answermen for knowing what to do and being the creative geniuses that they are. To Ryan and Susan Latrielle for their support and attention to detail to help create a book we are all proud of! Last but not least to Brad—who is the love of my life and the best decision I have ever made. I love you sweetheart! We have come a long way baby!

> *"For I know the plans I have for you ... to give you a future and a hope ... "*
> *Jeremiah 29:11*

Kathy Smart, *PTS, RSNA, RNC, Holistic Chef*

About Kathy

Kathy Smart is a TV Show Host, Chef and Nutritionist, a multi-award winning health expert, a diagnosed Celiac, and known as North America's leading gluten free expert. Kathy has appeared on such shows as Dr. Oz, CBC, Global, Rogers TV and CTV where she teaches, motivates and inspires others to live smarter by providing health recipes and healthy living tips specific for the wheat free and gluten free lifestyle.

 She is also the award recipient of the Ontario government's 2012 "Leading Women's Award" and named the National Health Activist of the Year for 2012 for bringing gluten free awareness across North America. Kathy travels acrossnorth America with the gluten Free Expo ~ Canada's largest gluten free expo bringing the world her wheat free and gluten free decadence.

As the host and chef of North America's first gluten free and vegetarian TV show "Live The Smart Way" on Rogers TV as well as the author of the bestseller Live The Smart Way Gluten-Free Cookbook.

Qualifications

- Applied Nutrition, Alive Academy of Natural Health, 2000
- Sports Nutrition, Alive Academy of Natural Health, 2004
- Registered Sports Nutrition Advisor, RSNA, 2004
- Anatomy and Physiology, Alive Academy of Natural Health, 2004
- Registered Nutritional Consultant, RNC,
- Canadian Examining Board of Health Care Professionals, 2006
- Biology, Alive Academy of Natural Health, 2007
- Registered Fitness Instructor Specialist, FIS, Canadian Fitness Professionals, 2007
- Personal Trainer Specialist, PTS, Canadian Fitness Professionals, 2004
- Holistic Cooking Academy of Canada, Holistic Teaching Chef
- Certificate of Plant Nutrition, eCornell University, 2011

Foreword by Don Warren

Every now and then you meet someone you just know will make a difference in life. Even young persons, who have not set the course for their lives will often reveal something in their character and personality that stands out, and you say to yourself…"Wait and see! This person is certain to make an impact with her life."

And so it has been with Kathy Smart. Taking challenges which she experienced as a young person with her health and eating, she has transformed those challenges into something positive and of benefit to many through her training, professional work and through her writing. This book is one of those positive "outcomes" that will benefit anyone who has struggled with how to make eating fun again when gluten has been identified as a food sensitivity.

Every day in my practice, I see children as well as adults whose health has been negatively impacted by the foods they eat. Unknowingly they are eating foods that their body does not tolerate well, often with significant health consequences. Once the food intolerances have been identified, and the diet is changed, often remarkable changes happen in the health of the child or adult.

One of the difficulties in making changes in one's diet is to find foods and recipes that are both nutritious and that please the taste buds. Kathy has accomplished this in her present cookbook. Not only has she given wonderful recipes based on her training as a nutritionist and chef, she has also laid out additional facts that inform the reader of the various attributes of the recipe (the "accolades" and nutritional analysis) and has also provided "Smart Facts" that give a rationale as to why the ingredients of the recipe are good for you. This cookbook will be welcome by those looking for a way to make eating enjoyable and nutritious while eliminating those foods that don't agree. It certainly has my recommendation.

Don Warren, N.D.

Don Warren is a Naturopathic Doctor with a family practice in Ottawa, Ontario. During his career as a doctor of naturopathic medicine, he has served as the president of the Canadian College of Naturopathic Medicine and is the immediate past president of the Council on Naturopathic Medical Education, the U.S. federally recognized accrediting agency for naturopathic medical education. He was a founding member of the Academic Consortium for Complementary and Alternative Medicine, (educators from the accredited and licensable CAM professions) and is a senior editor of a soon to be published textbook on naturopathic medicine. For several years, has been teaching in East Africa and is the founder of the Rwanda Selenium Supplementation trial. Don lives with his wife Barbara on their organic farm near Manotick. Eleven grandchildren keep them young and smiling.

Foreword by Adrian Delorey

I feel honored to be asked to contribute to the forward for the revision of this cutting edge cookbook. As an Entrepreneur & Kinesiologist, I always stress the importance of proper nutrition to my clients as it has always played a major role in the projects we develop. We have had thousands of clients come through our programs and I have witnessed first-hand the impact Kathy Smarts recipes and meal plans can have on the outcome of a fitness and lifestyle protocol. Over the past few years we have worked extensively together and I have come to know Kathy as not only a business partner but now see her as a close friend and one that shares an intense passion for helping others "Live The Smart Way". I feel I can open a window to you the reader as to who really is Kathy Smart; behind the scenes and away from the camera, and why you can trust in her recipes, guidance and advice.

Having worked in the fitness industry for over 16 years you come to know a few things. You can quickly determine the players from the pretenders and those who are truly walking the walk. Kathy Smart is not only in the arena she is leading the charge and it started with the very recipes in this book. Kathy's ability to make healthy food taste amazing is extraordinary and the additions to this book are nothing short of cutting edge. An entrepreneur has two choices, to copy and replicate or to innovate and create. This book and the additions Kathy has included represent the latter.

You hold in your hands more than just a Cookbook. You have a way of life. Recipes that were constructed with painstaking effort, infused with honesty & integrity, and a sprinkle of Kathy's zest for life in every single recipe. Very proud of you and this book fellow Health Renegader!

Adrian Delorey BSC(K), CK

Kinesiologist and Fitness Entrepreneur Adrian Delorey shares Smart's passion for educating others on the benefits of living a healthier lifestyle. The two recently launched a joint venture entitled Renegades of health which is designed to dispel common fitness and nutrition myths. Adrian has worked in the health and fitness industry since 1995 and is the owner of 180°Fitness training center. His credo in both business and life is to practice what you preach. Recipient of the Orleans Peoples Choice Business awards for Business Person of the Year 2007, Best Customer Service in 2008, and most recently the recipient of the Ottawa Health Leadership award in 2012. He has worked as a Kinesiologist, Phlebotomist, & Physio assistant at various hospitals throughout Halifax, Nova Scotia. Additionally, he had the rare opportunity to work in his field internationally. He has spent 3 months in Otse, a small village in Botswana, Africa. During his time there h visited the sick and dying (primarily those afflicted with HIV/Aids, worked with mentally and disabled youth & taught first aid.). Adrian has been continuing his education since 1997 and holds a 4 yr bachelor of science in Kinesiology degree as well as a 2 year honors conversion degree from Dalhousie University, in Nova Scotia www.180Fitness.ca

Foreword by William Davis

There are chefs who understand the art of clever food preparation. There are nutritionists who study the relationship of food to human health. But rarely are the two disciplines wedded. That unique combination of insights is what Kathy Smart does best: Uniting the lessons of nutrition with the aesthetics of a gourmet.

In her updated Live the Smart Way: Gluten-Free & Wheat-Free Cookbook, Ms. Smart takes this unique discipline one step further: She incorporates the lessons learned from the gluten-free experience for health into the mix, emerging with this glorious cookbook, a celebration of foods that are designed to be as nutritious as they are beautiful to behold and delicious to consume. By doing so, she shows the reader that the ideal lifestyle of eating fewer or no grains can be every bit as delicious and versatile as one that includes grains but compromises health.

Newcomers to the gluten-free lifestyle learn, via agonizing trial and error, that the methods of baking, for instance, are different from that of grain-based baking. This cookbook helps the reader and nascent gluten-free gourmet leapfrog past these hurdles, allowing you to create gluten-free works of art with your first efforts. That is indeed smart, isn't it?

William Davis, MD

Author of #1 New York Times Bestseller Wheat Belly: Lose the wheat, lose the weight and find your path back to health published by Rodale, Inc. Author, Track Your Plaque: The only heart disease prevention program that shows how the new CT heart scans can be used to detect, track, and control coronary plaque.

Blogs: www.wheatbellyblog.com, www.trackyourplaque.com/blog Founder, www.trackyourplaque.com

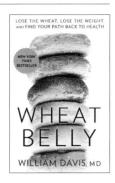

Table of Contents

Soups and Stews

Main Courses

Sides

Desserts or the 10 Percent Rule

Appendix

This cookbook is designed for those people who have several food sensitivities or food allergies. Each recipe has a "Recipe Highlights" section that points out specific recipe attributes that are defined in the back of this book. Each recipe has also been carefully analyzed and a complete nutritional breakdown has been done for those needing to calculate their fibre, carbohydrate and protein intake. We have also included a "Smart Facts" section for those that like a little information about the benefits or attributes about a certain ingredient.

Each recipe has been meticulously tested and retested for quality and consistency by friends, family, nutritionsits and chefs alike.

As I have a passion for both food and the environment, whenever possible I use fresh, local ingredients from our local farmers' markets and local stores. If I can inspire you to do the same and even plant a little herb garden—you won't regret it. The taste and quality of organic meats, eggs, vegetables and fruits will surpass your expectations!

May you enjoy this cookbook as much as I have enjoyed writing it!

May you be blessed with peace, abundance and happy cooking!

Breakfast

Breakfast truly is the most important meal of the day. A balanced breakfast will set the stage for your day, increasing your energy and your metabolism. Enjoy these balanced breakfast recipes.

List of recipes:

- Dark Chocolate Breakfast Cupcakes
- Flourless Cranberry Breakfast Muffins
- High Protein Pancakes
- Iron Rich Breakfast Mix
- Kathy's Breakfast Parfait
- Lemon Poppy Seed Muffins
- Peaches and Cream Steel Cut Oats
- The Ultimate Granola
- Zesty Spanish Omelette
- Metabolism Booster Coconut Flour Pancakes
- Chocolate Quinoa Breakfast Bars
- Smart Nutella
- Superfruit Granola Bars

Dark Chocolate Breakfast Cupcakes

These muffins are a definite hit wherever you may serve them. The ground almonds and whole eggs give a protein punch! This is a great way to get children to eat breakfast—a chocolate cupcake! *Serves 12*

Ingredients

- ¾ cup dark chocolate chips
- ½ cup unsweetened applesauce
- ½ cup butter or coconut oil
- 4 whole eggs—separate whites and yolks
- ½ cup pure maple syrup
- 1 teaspoon vanilla extract
- ½ teaspoon sea salt
- 1½ cups ground almonds
- 5 tablespoons gluten-free flour blend
- 2 teaspoons gluten-free baking powder

Glaze:

- ½ cup melted dark chocolate chips
- ¼ cup agave nectar
- 2 tablespoons brown rice syrup
- 1 teaspoon vanilla extract

Directions

Preheat oven to 350°F.

Melt chocolate chips, applesauce and butter/coconut oil over low heat.

Beat egg yolks with ¼ cup of the maple syrup and set aside.

Combine the melted chocolate mixture and egg yolk-maple syrup mixture together. Stir in ground almonds, vanilla extract, baking powder, sea salt and flour.

Beat 4 egg whites with the remaining ¼ cup of maple syrup until stiff. Fold into the above mixture.

☑ Smart Facts

Eating chocolate triggers the production of endorphins in the body which results in a feeling of happiness! Dark chocolate also contains appetite suppressant properties which help curb your appetite and cravings. Enjoy the hit of happiness and curb your cravings with these cupcakes!

RECIPE HIGHLIGHTS

* No Added Refined Sugars
* Vegeterian
* High in Protein

☑ Nutritional Analysis

Amount Per Serving	
Calories	224.39
Total Fat	15.81 g
Saturated Fat	6.6 g
Cholesterol	77.86 mg
Sodium	187.64 mg
Potassium	134.26 mg
Total Carbohydrates	18.91 g
Fibre	2.21 g
Sugar	7.4 g
Protein	4.79 g

Grease a muffin tin or line with muffin cups and fill each muffin tin until about ¾ full.

Bake for 20 minutes or until toothpick comes out clean.

Flourless Cranberry Breakfast Muffins

This is a colourful muffin perfect for those mornings when you need a quick, pick-me-up breakfast or snack. With each bite you have the explosion of tart cranberries contrasted perfectly with the richness of ground almonds, honey and butter. *Serves 12*

Ingredients

- 3 cups of ground almonds
- ½ teaspoon of baking soda
- ½ teaspoon of gluten-free baking powder
- ¼ teaspoon of sea salt
- 1½ teaspoon of cinnamon
- ½ teaspoon of lemon zest
- 3 whole eggs
- 1 teaspoon of vanilla extract
- ½ cup of honey
- 1½ cups of fresh or frozen cranberries

Optional Topping:
- 1 tablespoon of softened butter
- 2 tablespoons of honey

Directions

Preheat the oven to 325°F.

Line a muffin tin with large paper baking cups.

In a bowl, combine the almond flour, baking soda, baking powder, sea salt, cinnamon and lemon zest and mix well. In another bowl, whisk the eggs, honey, and vanilla then stir in the cranberries.

Gradually add the dry ingredients to the wet ingredients in three separate turns, mixing well after each addition.

Evenly fill each baking cup with the batter (fill to top of cup, muffin only rises about 1 to 1½ centimetres beyond cup) and bake in preheated oven for 18 to 20 minutes.

☑ Smart Facts

Almonds are a rich source of nutrients and monosaturated fats, which help to reduce the levels of LDL cholesterol and in turn the risk of heart disease. Almonds are also an excellent source of protein.

RECIPE HIGHLIGHTS

* Dairy Free
  (if topping is omitted)
* Simple and Quick
* Low Glycemic
* High in Protein and Fibre
* No Added Refined Sugars
* Vegetarian

☑ Nutritional Analysis

Amount Per Serving

Calories	241.85
Total Fat	15.88 g
Saturated Fat	3.1 g
Cholesterol	60.51 mg
Sodium	171.47 mg
Potassium	208.02 mg
Total Carbohydrates	21.87 g
Fibre	3.75 g
Sugar	16.11 g
Protein	10 g

Allow muffins to cool.

Combine butter and honey together and add to the tops of cooled muffins.

High Protein Pancakes

Protein first thing in the morning helps to stabilize blood sugar levels and increases metabolism. These pancakes are a great way to start the day or make a perfect pre or post workout snack. These pancakes also freeze well and can be toasted just before serving for a quick breakfast. *Makes 2 medium size pancakes*

Ingredients

- ½ cup of quick cooking gluten-free oatmeal
- ½ cup of cottage cheese
- 1 teaspoon of vanilla extract and cinnamon
- 2 eggs

Directions

Purée all ingredients in a blender.

Heat a non-stick skillet to medium, brush bottom lightly with butter or oil and fry pancakes on both sides until golden.

Top with your favourite pancake topping such as pure maple syrup, fresh berries, almond butter or yogurt.

☑ Smart Facts

Studies have shown that just ½ teaspoon of cinnamon daily can significantly reduce LDL (bad cholesterol).

Studies are also showing that cinnamon has regulatory effects on blood sugar levels—making it an excellent addition for anyone with diabetes Type 2 or any other blood sugar issues. These protein pancakes are an excellent way to balance your blood sugar by using both cinnamon and protein!

RECIPE HIGHLIGHTS

- * Simple and Quick
- * No Added Refined Sugars
- * Vegetarian
- * Low Glycemic
- * Diabetic Friendly

☑ Nutritional Analysis

Amount Per Serving	
Calories	189
Total Fat	6.9 g
Saturated Fat	2.1 g
Cholesterol	213.8 mg
Sodium	249 mg
Potassium	189 mg
Total Carbohydrates	15.6 g
Fibre	2.1 g
Sugar	2.07 g
Protein	16.7 g

Iron-Rich Breakfast Mix

I developed this recipe with many of my celiac and vegetarian clients in mind as a yummy way to get their daily iron without having to take a supplement. I often will tell clients to make large batches of this recipe to have on hand.
Serves 2

Ingredients

- 3 tablespoons of sesame seeds or hemp seeds
- 3 tablespoons of sunflower seeds
- 4 tablespoons of pistachio nuts
- 4 tablespoons of pumpkin seeds
- 4 tablespoons of gluten-free large flaked oats
- 2 tablespoons of chia seeds
- ½ teaspoon of cinnamon
- 2 tablespoons of blackstrap molasses (available at a health food store)
- ½ cup of pure apple juice

Directions

Combine all nuts, seeds and oats in a bowl. Add the cinnamon and mix well. Stir in the blackstrap molasses and add apple juice to the mixture stirring until all of the seeds and grains are coated.

Let stand for 15 minutes to allow the liquid to be absorbed into the seeds and grains.

☑ Smart Facts

Iron is an essential mineral that you need for good health throughout life. If you don't get enough iron you may feel tired, cold and have low energy. You may also look pale, be irritable and have trouble concentrating. Ask your family doctor for a blood test to determine if you have low iron.

RECIPE HIGHLIGHTS

* Simple and Quick
* Dairy Free
* High in Iron, Calcium and Fibre
* Low Glycemic
* Vegetarian and Vegan

☑ Nutritional Analysis

Amount Per Serving

Calories	238.46
Total Fat	15.17 g
Saturated Fat	2.12 g
Cholesterol	0 mg
Sodium	9.99 mg
Potassium	542.41 mg
Total Carbohydrates	21.65 g
Fibre	4.64 g
Sugar	4.29 g
Protein	7.31 g

Lemon Poppy Seed Muffins

I can remember my mother making these for a family picnic one year when we went to visit Upper Canada Village along the St. Lawrence River. I love how the lemon combines with the crunch of the poppy seeds. This is a great snack or breakfast! *Serves 6*

Ingredients

- 2 eggs, beaten
- 1 tablespoon of melted butter or coconut oil
- 3 tablespoons of honey
- 3 tablespoons of plain Greek yogurt
- 1 teaspoon of pure vanilla extract
- 1 tablespoon of lemon zest
- 2 tablespoons of freshly squeezed lemon juice
- ½ teaspoon of gluten-free baking powder
- 5 tablespoons of coconut flour
- 2 tablespoons of poppy seeds

  Glaze:
- 2 tablespoons of honey
- 1 teaspoon of butter

Directions

Preheat oven to 350°F.

Combine the first 7 ingredients in a medium size bowl stirring until well combined. Combine the baking powder and the coconut flour and add by spoonfuls to the liquid mixture until well combined.

Line a muffin tin with paper cups or lightly grease. Add batter to fill each cup.

Bake for 15-20 minutes or until toothpick comes out clean.

Allow muffins to cool, then remove from tins.

☑ Smart Facts

Coconut flour has the highest percentage of dietary fibre found in any flour—containing almost double the amount of fibre than wheat bran. Coconut flour consists of 58% dietary fibre where wheat bran contains only 27% fibre. You should aim for 25-35 grams of fibre per day to maintain a healthy weight, promote a feeling of fullness, balance blood sugar levels and eliminate toxins. Add coconut flour to your smoothies, and existing baked goods as an easy way to increase your fibre.

RECIPE HIGHLIGHTS

* Simple and Quick
* No Added Refined Sugars
* Vegetarian
* Low Glycemic

☑ Nutritional Analysis

Amount Per Serving	
Calories	166
Total Fat	8 g
Saturated Fat	4 g
Cholesterol	110 mg
Sodium	109 mg
Potassium	135 mg
Total Carbohydrates	18.5 g
Fibre	1 g
Sugar	15 g
Protein	4 g

Kathy's Breakfast Parfait

People often ask me what I eat for breakfast. This is one of my favourite mainstays and a breakfast that I enjoy eating with a mug of steaming, hot, organic coffee. *Serves 1*

Ingredients

- ½ cup of plain Greek yogurt
- ½ cup of fresh or frozen blueberries or blackberries
- 3-4 tablespoons of Ultimate Granola
- 1 teaspoon of pure maple syrup

Directions

In a large parfait glass, layer the yogurt, berries and granola. When finished, drizzle with pure maple syrup and enjoy this delicious breakfast with your favorite hot beverage.

☑ Smart Facts

Greek yogurt has a delicious thick, creamy taste, even the non-fat varieties, since it's strained to remove whey which also removes water. Greek yogurt packs a huge protein punch—containing 18-20 grams per ½ cup serving. Compared to the typical 8-10 grams of protein for regular yogurt, Greek yogurt is an excellent choice for a protein rich breakfast guaranteed to get that metabolism going!

RECIPE HIGHLIGHTS

* Simple and Quick
* No Added Refined Sugars
* Diabetic Friendly
* Egg Free
* Low Glycemic

☑ Nutritional Analysis

Amount Per Serving	
Calories	270
Fat	5 g
Saturated fat	0 g
cholesterol	0 mg
Sodium	10 mg
Potassium	240 mg
Total Carbohydrates	36.3 g
Fibre	5.5 g
Sugar	13 g
Protein	18.18 g

Peaches and Cream Steel Cut Oats

I love waking up to the smell of this simple and nutritious breakfast. The slow cooker makes having your steel cut oats in the morning a cinch! *Serves 4*

Ingredients

- 1 cup of gluten-free steel cut oats
- 4 cups of almond milk or cow's milk
- 1 teaspoon of pure vanilla extract
- 2 cups of fresh or frozen peaches

Optional Add In:

- chopped apricots, dates, almonds and a pinch of pumpkin pie spice for a nice change.

Directions

Add all of the above ingredients to a slow cooker and allow to cook on low for 6-8 hours or on high for 2-4 hours.

Add pure maple syrup and cinnamon to taste.

☑ Smart Facts

What is so great about steel cut oats? Steel cut oats are whole grain groats (the inner portion of the oat kernel) which have been cut into only two or three pieces by steel rather than being rolled. Steel cut oats have a lower glycemic index than instant oatmeal making it an excellent breakfast for anyone looking to increase their fibre or watching their waistline!

RECIPE HIGHLIGHTS

* Simple and Quick
* Dairy Free
* Diabetic Friendly
* No Added Refined Sugars
* High in Fibre
* Low Glycemic
* Vegetarian and Vegan

☑ Nutritional Analysis

Amount Per Serving	
Calories	187.77
Total Fat	1.51 g
Saturated Fat	0.48 g
Cholesterol	0 mg
Sodium	123.86 mg
Potassium	333.1 mg
Total Carbohydrates	34.17 g
Fibre	5.42 g
Sugar	7.53 g
Protein	7.72 g

The Ultimate Granola

This granola is absolutely chockful of nutrition! It has lots of fibre, protein and healthy monosaturated fats to keep you feeling full all morning long!

And the smell of this granola when cooking ... if heaven has a smell ... it has to smell like this!
Serves 20

Ingredients

- 1¼ cups of gluten-free steel cut oats
- 1¾ cups of gluten-free rolled oats
- 1 cup of gluten-free oat bran or rice bran
- ½ cup each of sunflower seeds, sesame seeds and walnut pieces
- ¼ cup of unsweetened shredded coconut, hemp seeds and pumpkin seeds
- ¾ cup each of pecans, peanuts with skins on and raw almonds
- ½ teaspoon of sea salt
- ⅓ cup of coconut oil or butter melted
- ½ cup of agave nectar or honey
- ½ cup of pure maple syrup
- 4 teaspoons of vanilla extract

Directions

Preheat oven to 250°F.

Mix all the dry ingredients together in a large bowl until well combined.

In a separate bowl, whisk together agave nectar/honey, maple syrup and vanilla extract.

Pour melted coconut oil over dry ingredients and mix well. Add the liquid mixture in and mix well.

Spread the mixture onto a parchment-lined baking sheet. Bake in oven, stirring every 15 minutes.

When granola is golden brown and very fragrant, (about 1 hour) remove from the oven and allow to cool.

☑ Smart Facts

Hemp seeds contain 6 immune boosting essential fatty acids in the perfect ratio for humans! Hemp seeds are composed of 65% of the most digestible form of protein for the human body. Hemp seeds reduce inflammation and improve the health of your skin and stimulate the growth of your hair, skin and nails.

RECIPE HIGHLIGHTS

* Simple and Quick
* Egg Free
* Vegetarian and Vegan
* No Added Refined Sugars
* High in Fibre
* Low Glycemic

☑ Nutritional Analysis

Amount Per ¼ Cup Serving

Calories	160
Total Fat	10 g
Saturated Fat	3 g
Cholesterol	0 mg
Sodium	4 mg
Potassium	170 mg
Total Carbohydrates	15 g
Fibre	3 g
Sugar	7 g
Protein	4 g

Store in airtight containers. Freezes very well and keeps up to 3 months.

Zesty Spanish Omelette

Eggs are an excellent way to kick-off your morning. This omelette is very tasty do to the combination of tomato and basil and the healthy kick of cayenne at the end of each bite. *Serves 4*

Ingredients

- 1 tablespoon of olive oil
- 2 chopped green onions
- ½ cubed green pepper
- 1 cubed red pepper
- 2 cloves of garlic, crushed
- 1 cup of fresh, diced tomatoes
- 1 teaspoon of dried basil
- 1 teaspoon of dried oregano
- ½ teaspoon of cayenne pepper
- Sea salt and pepper to taste
- 1 teaspoon of olive oil
- 6 organic eggs

Directions

Heat 1 teaspoon of olive oil in pan and sauté onions, peppers and garlic over medium high heat.

Add tomatoes, basil and oregano and let simmer for 5 minutes.

Put 1 teaspoon of olive oil in a separate pan over medium heat and add eggs. Cook until moist and fluffy.

Add tomato sauce and finish cooking over low heat for 3 minutes. Garnish with mozzarella or cheddar cheese if desired.

☑ Smart Facts

Eggs are one of the only foods that contain naturally occurring vitamin D!

Eggs promote healthy hair and nails because of their high sulphur content and wide array of vitamins and minerals. Many people find their hair grows faster after adding whole eggs to their diet.

RECIPE HIGHLIGHTS

* Easy to Make
* Dairy Free
* No Added Refined Sugars
* Low Glycemic
* Low in Saturated Fat
* Diabetic Friendly

☑ Nutritional Analysis

Amount Per Serving
Serving size: ¼ of a recipe

Calories	173.42
Total Fat	12.24 g
Saturated Fat	2.99 g
Cholesterol	317.25 mg
Sodium	142.8 mg
Potassium	303.88 mg
Total Carbohydrates	6.21 g
Fibre	1.91 g
Sugar	3.34 g
Protein	10.49 g

Metabolism Booster Coconut Flour Pancakes

I absolutely LOVE coconut flour- the taste is rich and the aroma like heaven while cooking. I also love coconut flour for the nutritional benefits of high fibre and metabolism stimulating properties .When people ask me what my favourite food is- I right away say pancakes! My mom would ask me every morning what I wanted for breakfast before school. And my answer was always pancakes! I can clearly remember me sitting down and eating pancakes almost every morning while she French braided my hair and my brother would make funny faces at me.

Makes 4 small pancakes

Ingredients

- 3 eggs
- 2 Tablespoons of melted coconut oil
- ¼ cup +1 Tablespoon of unsweetened vanilla almond milk
- 1 teaspoon of maple syrup
- ½ teaspoon sea salt
- 1 teaspoon cinnamon
- 3 tablespoons coconut flour
- 1 medium apple, shredded

Directions

Combine all ingredients except shredded apple in a bowl and blend until there are no clumps.

Fold in apple bits and stir to combine.

Cook in a preheated, greased skillet or pan over medium heat until golden on both sides. Pancakes are usually ready to flip when edges begin to look golden and bubbly.

☑ Smart Facts

What makes these pancakes boost my metabolism if they look high in fat?

Not all fats are created equal. Coconut oil and coconut flour have metabolism stimulating properties to the thyroid. Coconut products are medium chain triglyceride fats. These fats are not stored as body fat, but actually stimulate the metaboslim and are used by the liver as fuel! The high fibre content of these pancakes keep the blood sugar stable through out the day and that feature is boosted by the fat blasting properties of cinnamon. Enjoy!

☑ Nutritional Analysis

Amount Per Serving

Calories	177
Total Fat	12 g
Cholesterol	159.2 mg
Sodium	69.1 mg
Potassium	110.4 mg
Carbohydrates	7 g
Fiber	4 g
Sugar	4.6 g
Protein	7.7 g

Chocolate Quinoa Breakfast Bars

These breakfast bars are moist and filled with protein due to the base of quinoa and eggs. Coconut oil adds a metabolism boosting benefit to stimulate the thyroid too! Chocolate for breakfast anyone? *Serves 12*

Ingredients

- ²/₃ cup white or golden quinoa
- 1¹/₃ cups water
- ¹/₃ cup of unsweetened vanilla almond milk
- 4 Large eggs
- 1 teaspoon vanilla extract
- ¾ cup coconut oil
- 1 ¼ cups coconut sugar
- 1 cup unsweetened cocoa powder
- 1 ½ teaspoons each of baking powder, baking soda and sea salt

Directions

Bring the quinoa and water to a boil in a medium saucepan. Cover, reduce to a simmer and cook for 10 minutes. Turn off the heat, and leave the covered saucepan on the burner for another 10 minutes. Fluff with a fork, and allow the quinoa to cool.

Preheat the oven to 350 degrees. Thoroughly grease a baking pan.

Combine the milk, eggs and vanilla in a blender or food processor. Add the 2 cups of cooked quinoa and coconut oil and continue to blend until smooth.

Combine the sugar, cocoa, baking powder, baking soda, and salt in a medium bowl. Add the contents from the blender and mix well.

Divide the batter evenly between the 12 muffin cups.

Bake on the center oven rack for 30 to 35

minutes, or until a knife inserted into the center comes out clean.

Cool completely and store in a sealed container in the refrigerator for up to one week, or freeze for up to one month.

☑ Smart Facts

Coconut sugar, derived from the flowers of the coconut tree, is an organic, sustainable natural sweetener that shows promising results for people who suffer from chronic illnesses or conditions such as diabetes, gallstones, cancer, heart disease and obesity. This sugar has a low glycemic index and is also a nutrient powerhouse, filled with lots of vitamins, minerals and amino acids.

RECIPE HIGHLIGHTS

* Dairy Free
* Gluten-Free
* Vegetarian
* Diabetic Friendly

☑ Nutritional Analysis

Amount Per Serving	
Calories	198.19
Total Fat	10.85g
Saturated Fat	8.53g
Cholesterol	101.54mg
Sodium	320.91mg
Potassium	199.73mg
Total Carbohydrates	15.61g
Fiber	3.04g
Sugar	16.63g
Protein	5.18g

Smart Nutella

A Smart Twist on a classic!

Delicious spread on a wholegrain gluten-free toast with sliced strawberries. Sure to be a hit with the whole family! *Makes ¾ cup*

Ingredients

- ½ cup of almond hazelnut nut butter
- ¼ cup of pure maple syrup (or to taste as some children like it sweeter)
- 4 Tablespoons of unsweetened cocoa
- ¼ tsp fine sea salt

Directions

Mix the above ingredients thoroughly and store in fridge until needed.

☑ Nutritional Analysis

Amount Per Tablespoon

Calories	112
Total Fat	8.1g
Cholesterol	0mg
Sodium	74.6mg
Potassium	118.3mg
Carbohydrates	7.7g
Fiber	<1g
Sugar	4.5g
Protein	4g

☑ Smart Facts

Almond hazelnut butter is an elegant tasting nut butter that packs in all the nutrition of whole almonds and hazelnuts.

Almonds are high in potassium, magnesium, phosphorus and protein.

Almond hazelnut butter contains 8 grams of protein per 2 tablespoon serving, heart healthy monounsaturated fat and 0 cholesterol.

Almond hazelnut butter concentrates the sweet, pleasant flavour of almonds and hazelnuts and can be used anywhere peanut butter is called for.

Almond hazelnut butter can be found in your natural foods section of your local grocery store, health food store or bulk food store.

RECIPE HIGHLIGHTS

* Dairy Free
* Easy to Make
* Egg Free
* Gluten and Wheat Free
* High in Protein
* No Added Refined Sugars
* Vegan/ Vegetarian

Cranberry Blueberry Granola Bars

This is an excellent gluten-free alternative to granola bars. The seeds make this recipe both high in protein and fibre.

18 Servings

Ingredients

- 1 cup gluten-free oats
- 1/3 cup each of pecans, pumpkin seeds and sesame seeds
- 1/2 cup unsweetened almond butter, cashew butter, peanut butter or sunflower seed butter
- 1/2 cup honey
- 1 teaspoon vanilla extract
- 4 tablespoons ground flax seeds
- 1/4 cup each of dried blueberries, cranberries, cherries and golden raisins
- 1/3 cup of unsweetened coconut flakes
- 1/2 teaspoon sea salt
- 1 teaspoon lemon juice
- Coconut oil to grease baking sheet

Directions

Preheat oven to 325.

Pulse all of the ingredients in a food processor until coarsely chopped. Grease a 9 inch by 9 inch pan with the coconut oil. Pour the mixture into pan and bake in the oven for 20-25 minutes. Remove from oven and let cool. When completely cooled, cut into bars.

☑ Smart Facts

Sunflower Seeds contain" Chlorogenic acid" which is a powerful antioxidant found in in all plant leaves and stems- including the sunflower. Under certain baking conditions, this acid causes the baked good to turn "green." To eliminate this effect, add lemon juice to any recipe that calls for sunflower seeds or sunflower butter.

RECIPE HIGHLIGHTS

* Dairy Free
* High in Fibre
* No Added Refined Sugars
* Gluten and Wheat Free
* Egg Free
* Low Glycemic

☑ Nutritional Analysis

Amount Per Serving		
Calories		195
Calories From Fat (42%)		82
% Daily Value		
Total Fat	10.45g	16%
Saturated Fat	3.19g	16%
Cholesterol	0mg	0%
Sodium	41.99mg	2%
Potassium	177.92mg	5%
Total Carbohydrates	27.84g	9%
Fiber	3.12g	12%
Sugar	9.62g	
Protein	3.83g	8%

Salads

Research continually praises the importance of vegetables for fighting cancer, heart disease and obesity. Greens do not have to be bland or boring! Enjoy these salads as a side or even a main dish.

List of recipes:

- Almond Avocado Chicken with Red Pepper Salad
- Asparagus Salad
- Baby Spinach and Strawberry Summer Salad
- Cool California Salad
- Easy Chickpea Salad
- Grilled Tricolour Pepper salad
- High Protein Quinoa Salad
- Maple Mustard Salad Greens
- Mixed Greens with Dried Cherries and Goat Cheese
- Pesto Pasta Salad
- Spring Pear and Feta Salad
- Warm Beef Spring Salad
- Yummy, Yummy Thai Salad
- Juicy Red Watermelon and Olive Salad

Almond Avocado Chicken with Red Pepper Salad

Simple enough for everyday, but sophisticated enough for a special occasion! *Serves 4*

Ingredients

- 4 boneless, skinless chicken breasts
- ½ cup of roasted almonds, ground
- 1 egg
- ½ teaspoon of sea salt and pepper
- 2 teaspoons of olive oil

Salad Dressing:

- 1 ripe avocado
- 1 green onion, sliced fine
- 1 tablespoon of olive oil
- 3-4 tablespoons of water or chicken stock
- 3 tablespoons of fresh lime juice
- Pinch of ground coriander and ground cumin
- 1 clove of garlic, crushed

Salad:

- 1 head of Boston lettuce
- 1 each of yellow, red and orange peppers
- Juice of one lime

Directions

Preheat oven to 375°F.

Mix ground almonds, sea salt and pepper on a large plate. In a bowl, beat the egg until foamy. Dip the chicken breasts into the egg and then press both sides of the chicken into nut mixture. Heat olive oil in oven proof pan on medium heat, until hot. Sear chicken on each side until golden, about 5 minutes per side. Remove from heat and bake in oven until meat thermometer reaches 347-356°F and juices run clear.

Prepare the dressing:

Purée onion, avocado, lime juice, olive oil and spices in a blender. Thin with stock or water until desired consistency is achieved.

Prepare the salad:

Slice the peppers into julienne, add lime juice and allow to marinate while chicken is cooking.

Slice chicken breast. Fill four plates with lettuce and place sliced chicken on top of lettuce, allowing 1 breast for each plate. Top with julienne of peppers.

Spoon dressing over chicken and lettuce.

☑ Smart Facts

RECIPE HIGHLIGHTS
* Dairy Free
* Diabetic Friendly
* Easy to Make
* High in Protein
* Low Glycemic
* No Added Refined Sugars

☑ Nutritional Analysis

Amount Per Serving

Calories	395.22
Total Fat	23.1 g
Saturated Fat	3.48 g
Cholesterol	73.1 mg
Sodium	251.68 mg
Potassium	977.09 mg
Total Carbohydrates	13.83 g
Fibre	8.43 g
Sugar	3.11 g
Protein	33.41 g

Asparagus Salad

Asparagus is one of my favourite vegetables!
A sure sign of spring, I look forward to buying
fresh asparagus on St. Joseph's Blvd from our
local farmer. Picked only hours before eating!
Serves 6

Ingredients

- 4 cups of cooked asparagus, cut in ½ inch pieces
- 1 cup of chopped grape tomatoes
- ¼ cup of chopped red onion
- ¼ cup of crumbled feta cheese
- 2 tablespoons of fresh lemon juice
- 1 teaspoon of dried oregano
- 1 teaspoon of olive oil
- ¼ teaspoon of sea salt

Directions

Steam asparagus until crisp tender.

In a bowl, whisk together lemon juice, olive oil
and sea salt. Add cheese, onions and tomatoes.
Add asparagus while still hot and toss with
other salad ingredients.

Allow to stand until warm, toss again and serve
while asparagus is still warm.

☑ Smart Facts

Asparagus prevents the
formation of kidney stones,
cleanses the body and
detoxifies kidneys. Asparagus
also helps to prevent urinary
tract infections.

Asparagus can be used as an
aphrodisiac to enhance sexual
activity and helps to relieve
diarrhea and constipation.
Asparagus helps to strengthen
capillaries thus preventing
painful varicose veins.

RECIPE HIGHLIGHTS

* Simple and Quick
* No Added Refined Sugars
* Diabetic Friendly
* Vegetarian

☑ Nutritional Analysis

Amount Per Serving	
Calories	69.37
Total Fat	3.49 g
Saturated Fat	1.61 g
Cholesterol	8.34 mg
Sodium	206.58 mg
Potassium	309.38 mg
Total Carbohydrates	7.58 g
Fibre	2.57 g
Sugar	1.75 g
Protein	3.99 g

Baby Spinach and Strawberry Summer Salad

I have picked strawberries with my mom since I was 4 years old at Avonmore Berry Farm. This salad was created after I took my niece Ella there. I love the sweetness of the fresh strawberries and how it contrasts with the crunch of the pecans. *Serves 4*

Ingredients

- 1 teaspoon of olive oil
- 4 tablespoons of pecan halves
- 3 tablespoons of olive oil
- 2 tablespoons of balsamic vinegar
- 4 cups of washed baby spinach
- 1 cup of sliced strawberries
- 4 tablespoons of crumbled goat feta cheese

Directions

Toast pecan halves with 1 teaspoon of olive oil over medium heat until brown. Set aside.

In a small bowl, add vinegar and whisk in olive oil until emulsified.

Divide baby spinach between 4 plates. Top each plate with sliced strawberries, and garnish with crumbled feta cheese and toasted pecans. Drizzle with vinaigrette just before serving.

☑ Smart Facts

Multiple studies have validated spinach's ability to protect against cancer! Spinach is a good source of B2-riboflavin, which is proven to lessen the risk of cancer and helps the body cope with stress. Another key nutrient found in spinach, folate, helps prevent birth defects, certain cancers and heart disease.

RECIPE HIGHLIGHTS

* Simple and Quick
* Diabetic Friendly
* Low Glycemic
* No Added Refined Sugar
* Vegetarian
* High in Iron

☑ Nutritional Analysis

Amount Per Serving	
Calories	160.75
Total Fat	17.42 g
Saturated Fat	3.79 g
Cholesterol	8.34 mg
Sodium	130.96 mg
Potassium	310.16 mg
Total Carbohydrates	7.69 g
Fibre	2.51 g
Sugar	4.16 g
Protein	4.41 g

Cool California Salad

I absolutely adore avocados! Anytime I can add them into something, I do. (Yes, I have come up with some pretty weird combinations.) The richness of the avocado contrasts with the sweet clementines and salty feta to give you a salad you cannot stop eating. My father is a meat and potatoes kinda dad and he cannot get enough of this one! *Serves 8*

Ingredients

- 6 cups of baby spinach
- 1 whole avocado, peeled and cut into bite size chunks
- 1 can of baby clementine oranges cut into small thirds, drained
- OR 1 orange peeled, and sectioned with pith removed and cut into thirds
- ¼ cup of red onion, chopped
- 1 cup of cucumber, peeled and cut into bite size pieces
- ¼ cup of feta cheese, crumbled or tofu if dairy intolerant
- 1 red pepper cut into bite size pieces
- 1 tablespoon of olive oil
- 1 tablespoon of pure maple syrup
- 1 tablespoon of balsamic vinegar

Directions

Combine all of the vegetables and fruit into a large bowl. Stir in the avocado and feta cheese until evenly distributed. (The avocado will start to blend into the veggies and that is okay).

In a separate bowl whisk the olive oil, maple syrup and the balsamic vinegar for 1 minute and then add the dressing to the salad. Stir well until all vegetables are combined and coated with dressing.

Chill salad before serving.

☑ Smart Facts

The high fat content of the avocado is actually a good thing. According to studies done on the use of avocado in a diet to reduce cholesterol, it was determined that the monounsaturated fat in avocados helps to reduce triglyceride levels and increase HDL, which is the good cholesterol that helps to decrease the bad cholesterol. The monosaturated fat in the avocado is also good for treating dry skin, eczema and promotes shiny, healthy hair!

RECIPE HIGHLIGHTS

* Simple and Quick
* No Added Refined Sugars
* Low Glycemic
* Diabetic Friendly
* High in Iron
* Vegetarian and Vegan (if using tofu)

☑ Nutritional Analysis

Amount Per Serving

Calories	99.26
Total Fat	6.26 g
Saturated Fat	1.42 g
Cholesterol	4.17 mg
Sodium	74.14 mg
Potassium	378.12 mg
Total Carbohydrates	9.83 g
Fibre	3.23 g
Sugar	5.59 g
Protein	2.41 g

Easy Chickpea Salad

This salad is one of those recipes I make when I need a healthy lunch–fast! This recipe only takes a couple of minutes to make but keeps you satisfied for hours. *Serves 6*

Ingredients

- 1 can of chickpeas, drained and rinsed
- ½ cup of chopped celery, red apple and carrot
- 1 teaspoon of fresh lime juice
- 1 teaspoon of olive oil
- Sea salt and pepper to taste

Directions

Combine all of the above ingredients in a bowl and serve.

You can add in crumbled feta cheese, tofu or sliced avocado as well.

☑ Smart Facts

RECIPE HIGHLIGHTS
* Simple and Quick
* Dairy Free
* Diabetic Friendly
* Egg Free
* High in Fibre
* Low Glycemic
* No Added Refined Sugars
* Vegetarian and Vegan

☑ Nutritional Analysis

Amount Per Serving	
Calories	146
Total Fat	2.28 g
Saturated Fat	0.29 g
Cholesterol	0 mg
Sodium	295.44 mg
Potassium	296.93 mg
Total Carbohydrates	27.6 g
Fibre	5.6 g
Sugar	4.84 g
Protein	4.84 g

Grilled Tricolour Pepper Salad

This recipe is just as tasty as it is colourful! Enjoy the combination of garlic and feta cheese enhanced by fresh basil leaves. *Serves 4*

Ingredients

- 1 each large red, yellow and green bell peppers cut into quarters; seeded and peeled.
- 2 tablespoons of extra virgin olive oil
- 3 tablespoons of balsamic vinegar
- 2 cloves of garlic, minced
- ½ teaspoon of sea salt
- ¼ teaspoon of pepper
- ¼ cup of crumbled light feta cheese or tofu
- ¼ cup of sliced fresh basil leaves

Directions

Place bell peppers skin side down on BBQ over medium-high heat or place on baking sheet under the broiler in the oven. Cook 10-12 minutes or until skin is charred. Place peppers in a paper bag. Close bag and set aside and let cool for 10-15 minutes. Remove charred skin from peppers with knife and discard. Cut peppers in quarters, remove the white pith and any seeds and discard.

Place peppers in a glass serving dish. Combine oil, vinegar, garlic, sea salt and pepper in a small bowl. Whisk until well combined. Pour vinaigrette over bell peppers and let stand 30 minutes at room temperature.

Sprinkle with cheese (or tofu) and basil just before serving.

☑ Smart Facts

Red Peppers are high in vitamins A, C, E and selenium. These vitamins are essential in nourishing our immune system! A single red pepper has the equivalent vitamin C of 1 cup of orange juice!

RECIPE HIGHLIGHTS

* Simple and Quick
* Egg Free
* High in Antioxidants
* No Added Refined Sugars
* Low Glycemic
* Diabetic Friendly

☑ Nutritional Analysis

Amount Per Serving	
Calories	126.46
Total Fat	9.02 g
Saturated Fat	2.38 g
Cholesterol	8.34 mg
Sodium	346.2 mg
Potassium	251.77 mg
Total Carbohydrates	9.24 g
Fibre	1.81 g
Sugar	4.6 g
Protein	2.62 g

High Protein Quinoa Salad

When I first found out that I had to remove gluten from my diet this was one of the first recipes I developed using quinoa. It has since become a favourite with friends and family.
Serves 4

Ingredients

- 1 cup quinoa, rinsed
- 1½ cups of cold water
- ½ teaspoon sea salt
- 3 tablespoons each of fresh lemon and lime juice
- ½ teaspoon of sea salt
- ½ teaspoon of tabasco sauce
- ½ cup of kernelled corn
- 1 small red onion minced
- 1 small jalapeno minced or ½ teaspoon of red pepper flakes
- 1 red pepper finely diced
- 3 green scallions, minced
- ¼ cup of fresh cilantro, chopped
- 2 tablespoons of minced chives

Directions

Bring water to a boil and add ½ teaspoon sea salt and quinoa. Return mixture to a boil, cover and reduce heat to low and simmer for 15 minutes. Turn off heat and keep pot covered for 5 minutes. Spread quinoa on a tray to cool.

In a large bowl, whisk lemon and lime juices with tabasco sauce and sea salt until well combined. Add all vegetables and herbs, mixing thoroughly. Add cooked quinoa and toss until thoroughly combined.

Adjust seasoning, adding sea salt, pepper and fresh lime juice as desired.

☑ Smart Facts

Thoroughly rinse uncooked quinoa under cold running water to prevent it from having a bitter flavour.

RECIPE HIGHLIGHTS

* Simple and Quick
* Egg Free
* Dairy Free
* High Protein
* High Fibre
* No Added Refined Sugar
* Vegan and Vegetarian

☑ Nutritional Analysis

Amount Per Serving

Calories	137.36
Total Fat	1.97 g
Saturated Fat	0.23 g
Cholesterol	0 mg
Sodium	300 mg
Potassium	301.25 mg
Total Carbohydrates	25.92 g
Fibre	3.56 g
Sugar	2.03 g
Protein	5.11 g

Mixed Greens with Dried Cherries and Goat Cheese

My clients often become more like family to me than anything. This recipe comes from a very dear "family" client of mine, Janet, who made this salad when she was reducing her bread intake and increasing her vegetables while working with me. She proudly made this salad for me to try one day and I am so thankful for this recipe—I love it! *Serves 6*

Ingredients

- 4 cups of baby spinach or mixed greens
- 1 apple, chopped into bite size pieces
- ½ cup of dried cherries
- ½ cup of crumbled goat feta cheese
- ½ cup of walnuts
- ½ cup of diced celery
- 1 tablespoon of balsamic vinegar
- 1 tablespoon of olive oil

Directions

Toss all ingredients in a large salad bowl and serve.

☑ Smart Facts

Roasting walnuts brings out the complex flavours in the nuts. Roast them by placing in a pan on medium high heat for 1-2 minutes.

Walnuts are also an excellent source of heart healthy Omega 3 fatty acids.

RECIPE HIGHLIGHTS

* Easy to Make
* Low Glycemic
* No added Refined Sugars
* Vegetarian
* High in Omega 3 Fatty Acids
* Diabetic Friendly

☑ Nutritional Analysis

Amount Per Serving	
Calories	177.04
Total Fat	11.53 g
Saturated Fat	2.79 g
Cholesterol	11.13 mg
Sodium	153.61 mg
Potassium	163.35 mg
Total Carbohydrates	16.52 g
Fibre	2.55 g
Sugar	3.74 g
Protein	4.11 g

Pesto Pasta Salad

This salad is a perfect dish to bring to a dinner party or for entertaining. The garlic, olives, pesto and feta blend perfectly and keep you going back for seconds! *Serves 6*

Ingredients

- 6 cups of cooked brown rice pasta
- 3-4 cloves of garlic, crushed
- 1 teaspoon of white vinegar
- ¼ cup of extra virgin olive oil
- ½ red onion, chopped fine
- ½ jar of small olives, sliced thin 3 ounces
- ¼ cup of pesto
- ½ cup of light feta cheese, crumbled*
- 1 bunch of parsley, chopped fine

Directions

Cook the pasta according to package directions, rinse pasta well.

While pasta is cooking, prepare the vinaigrette. In a bowl, add crushed garlic, vinegar and slowly whisk in olive oil until mixture is emulsified. Add onions, olives and pesto, mixing until combined.

Add hot pasta to the bowl and toss. While still warm add the feta cheese, and chopped parsley, tossing until well combined. Salad can be served warm, or can be chilled in refrigerator and served cold.

Crumbled goat feta or crumbled firm tofu can be substituted for feta cheese if dairy intolerant/vegan.

☑ Smart Facts

Did you know parsley contains 3 x more vitamin C than oranges? Parsley is also an excellent remedy for edema or water retention, acting as a natural diuretic.

RECIPE HIGHLIGHTS

* Simple and Quick
* Dairy Free (if using tofu)
* Diabetic Friendly
* Egg Free
* High in Fibre
* Low Glycemic
* No Added Refined Sugars
* Vegetarian and Vegan (if using tofu)

☑ Nutritional Analysis

Amount Per Serving	
Calories	385.82
Total Fat	9.87 g
Saturated Fat	6.58 g
Cholesterol	25.13 mg
Sodium	350 mg
Potassium	176.59 mg
Total Carbohydrates	42.21 g
Fibre	7.59 g
Sugar	2.25 g
Protein	13.32 g

Maple Mustard Salad Greens

I just love this simple salad recipe! *Serves 4*

Ingredients

- 1 tablespoon of pure maple syrup
- 1 tablespoon of balsamic vinegar
- 1 teaspoon of honey Dijon mustard
- 2 tablespoons of fresh lime juice
- 3 tablespoons of extra virgin olive oil
- ½ teaspoon of dried oregano
- Sea salt and pepper to taste
- 1 pound of organic mixed salad greens

Directions

In a bowl, add maple syrup, vinegar, mustard and lime juice. Whisk together until well combined. Slowly whisk in olive oil until salad dressing is emulsified. Add oregano, and season to taste with sea salt and pepper. Let stand for 1 minute for flavourss to infuse.

In a large bowl, toss salad greens with dressing, serve immediately.

☑ Smart Facts

RECIPE HIGHLIGHTS
- * Dairy Free
- * Easy to Make
- * No Added Refined Sugars
- * Low Glycemic
- * Vegetarian

☑ Nutritional Analysis

Amount Per Serving

Calories:	110
Total Fat	10.2 g
Cholesterol	0 mg
Sodium	6.2 mg
Potassium	87.9 mg
Carbohydrates	5 g
Fibre	<1 g
Sugar	4.1 g
Protein	<1 g

Warm Beef Spring Salad

This is one of my favourite recipes that I make when I have company. The combination of the warm and tender beef with the crunch of the spring greens will impress any guest! *Serves 2*

Ingredients

- 2 4-ounce pieces of flank steak cut 1 inch thick
- 1 teaspoon of olive oil
- 1 tablespoon of Montreal Steak Spice* or black pepper
- 4 tablespoons of balsamic vinegar
- 2 tablespoons of olive oil
- Sea salt and pepper to taste
- 4-6 cups of spring greens (mesclun mix or field greens)
- ½ red pepper, sliced thin

Directions

Brush steak with the olive oil and rub in Montreal Steak Spice or black pepper.

Grill or BBQ meat until medium rare, (typically about 6-8 minutes) turning once.

Take the steak off the grill and allow to rest for 5 minutes under foil tent. While steak is resting, whisk together oil and vinegar and season to taste with sea salt and pepper.

Arrange spring greens on plates.

Thinly slice each piece of beef against the grain and place on top of the spring greens. Add the sliced red pepper and drizzle with the vinaigrette.

Serve with a baked sweet potato.

* Ensure the steak spice is gluten-free

☑ Smart Facts

RECIPE HIGHLIGHTS

- * Simple and Quick
- * Dairy Free
- * High Protein
- * No Added Refined Sugar
- * High in iron

☑ Nutritional Analysis

Amount Per Serving

Calories	430.08
Total Fat	29.6 g
Saturated Fat	6.8 g
Cholesterol	69.06 mg
Sodium	383.2 mg
Potassium	609.38 mg
Total Carbohydrates	9.88 g
Fibre	2.3 g
Sugar	6.31 g
Protein	28.74 g

Spring Pear and Feta Salad

Whenever I serve guests this salad, I can always expect a request for the recipe.
Serves 8

Ingredients

Salad Dressing:

- 2 tablespoons of apple cider vinegar
- 3 tablespoons of honey
- ½ teaspoon each of prepared mustard, dried thyme, celery salt and pepper
- ½ cup olive oil

Salad:

- 4 cups of spring mixed salad greens
- ½ cup each of green, red and orange peppers, sliced thin
- ⅓ cup of sliced green onions
- 4 fresh pears—peeled and sliced*
- ½ cup of crumbled feta cheese (or crumbled tofu)

Candied Pecans:

- ⅓ cup of pecan halves
- 1 tablespoon of pure maple syrup
- 1 teaspoon of butter

Directions

Prepare the vinaigrette: in a bowl, pour in vinegar, honey, mustard and spices, whisk until incorporated. Slowly add the olive oil whisking constantly until vinaigrette is emulsified.

In a non stick skillet, melt the butter, add the maple syrup and pecans. Toast carefully until lightly browned and fragrant.

Divide the salad mix over the 8 plates. Top with peppers, onions, and pear slices. Sprinkle on the crumbled feta and roasted pecans. Drizzle vinaigrette on top and garnish with small sprig of fresh thyme.

☑ Smart Facts

Apple cider vinegar has often been touted as being helpful for weight loss! According to a study published in the *Journal of Bioscience, Biotechnology and Biochemistry* showed that both body fat and the serum triglyceride levels decreased in the subjects taking 30ml of apple cider vinegar with breakfast compared to those taking just water. I often tell my clients to take 1 tablespoon of apple cider vinegar before meals to aid in both digestion and weight loss!

RECIPE HIGHLIGHTS

* Simple and Quick
* Dairy Free (if using tofu)
* Egg Free
* No Added Refined Sugars
* Vegetarian

☑ Nutritional Analysis

Amount Per Serving	
Calories	243.97
Total Fat	19.43 g
Saturated Fat	3.87 g
Cholesterol	9.62 mg
Sodium	215.99 mg
Potassium	190.61 mg
Total Carbohydrates	17.52 g
Fibre	2.52 g
Sugar	12.66 g
Protein	2.57 g

If pears are not in season, substitute with canned pears packed in juice.

Juicy Red Watermelon and Olive Salad

I know I know...before you turn the page ~ this is a recipe you NEED to try to believe... The first time I tried this was in a small, non assuming open restaurant on the beaches of Anguilla with my husband and your best friends Anne and Al. The chef was from Canada and made this salad and all I have to say ~ wow! The salty sweet and fresh combination of ingredients will have you making this every day for at least a week! *Serves 4*

Ingredients

- 4 cups of chopped fresh watermelon
- 1/8 cup sliced green olives
- 4 Tablespoons of crumbled feta cheese
- 1 Tablespoon of both olive oil and balsamic vinegar

Directions

Combine all of the above ingredients until well combined...smile and get ready.

☑ Smart Facts

Alongside of tomatoes, watermelon has moved up to the front of the line in recent research studies on high-lycopene foods. Lycopene is a carotenoid phytonutrient that's especially important for our cardiovascular health, and an increasing number of scientists now believe that lycopene is important for bone health as well.

RECIPE HIGHLIGHTS

* Easy to Make
* Gluten-Free
* No Added Refined Sugars
* Vegetarian
* Egg Free
* Diabetic Friendly

☑ Nutritional Analysis

Amount Per Serving	
Calories	108.76
Total Fat	6.06g
Saturated Fat	1.95g
Cholesterol	8.34mg
Sodium	145.49mg
Potassium	180.92mg
Total Carbohydrates	12.81g
Fiber	0.75g
Sugar	10.41g
Protein	2.31g

Yummy, Yummy Thai Salad

This is a simple salad recipe that has just the right amount of crunch from the brown rice and bean sprouts. The Thai inspired taste has just a hint of ginger heat at the end of each bite. *Serves 8*

Ingredients

Salad Dressing:

- 1 tablespoon of toasted sesame oil, fresh lime juice and grated fresh ginger
- 1 teaspoon of red pepper flakes and minced garlic
- 2 teaspoons of wheat-free tamari sauce

Salad:

- 2 cups of cooked brown basmati rice
- 2½ cups of bean sprouts
- 1 cup each of baby bok choy, chopped fine, chopped red pepper and chopped celery
- ½ cup each of chopped green pepper, chopped green onions and chopped almonds or peanuts

Directions

Whisk all of the dressing ingredients together in a small bowl. Set aside.

In a separate large bowl, combine the rice, vegetables and chopped almonds.

Slowly add the dressing to the salad, one tablespoonful at a time, gently stirring to ensure all vegetables are well coated.

For enhanced flavour, cook the brown rice in vegetable stock.

☑ Smart Facts

Bok Choy is a member of the brassica family of vegetables. Bok Choy has similar benefits to other cabbages in that it contains high amounts of nitrogen compounds called indoles that are photochemicals that are believed to deactivate potent estrogens that can stimulate the growth of tumours in the breast.

RECIPE HIGHLIGHTS

* Simple and Quick
* Dairy Free
* No Added Refined Sugars
* Low Glycemic
* Vegetarian and Vegan

☑ Nutritional Analysis

Amount Per Serving	
Calories	144.41
Total Fat	6.84 g
Saturated Fat	0.71 g
Cholesterol	0 mg
Sodium	100.82 mg
Potassium	275.57 mg
Total Carbohydrates	17.81 g
Fibre	3.47 g
Sugar	3.05 g
Protein	4.73 g

Soups and Stews

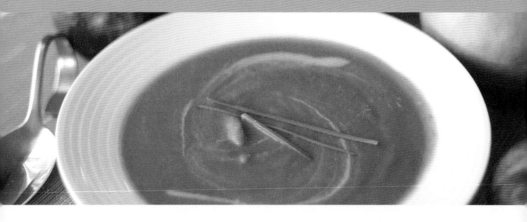

I truly do not know if there is anything more comforting than a bowl of steaming homemade soup. These soups are a way to have a "hug in a bowl" and an easy way to increase your daily serving of those important vegetables!

List of recipes:

- Butternut Squash and Banana Soup
- Citrus Infused Carrot Soup
- Creamy Cauliflower Soup
- Creamy Fennel Soup
- Curried Butternut Squash and Apple Soup
- Curried Pear and Parsnip Soup
- Homemade Chicken or Vegetable Soup Stock
- Homemade Vegan Soup Stock
- Roasted Asparagus Soup
- Smokey Red Pepper Soup
- Spicy Black Bean Chili
- Thai Inspired Vegan Stew
- Fresh, Moist and Chewy Gluten-Free Bread
- Creamy Broccoli Soup

Citrus Infused Carrot Soup

The subtle taste of orange zest in this recipe always keeps guests wondering what that special taste is. Another perfect soup for a cold day. *Serves 8*

Ingredients

- 1 tablespoon of butter/coconut oil
- 1 pound of carrots, chopped
- 1 cup of leeks, chopped
- 1 medium orange
- ¼ teaspoon of nutmeg
- 6 cups of vegetable broth
- 8 tablespoons of yogurt
- Fresh cilantro to garnish
- Sea salt and pepper to taste

Directions

Melt butter over medium heat in a large soup pot. Add carrots and leeks and cook gently for 10 minutes allowing the vegetables to soften.

Grate orange peel on a cheese grater to collect 2 tablespoons of orange zest.

Cut the orange in half, juice both halves and add juice and orange zest to the vegetables.

Add the vegetable stock and nutmeg to vegetables. Let the soup simmer uncovered for 30 minutes over low heat.

Purée with an immersion blender.

Add sea salt and pepper to taste.

☑ Smart Facts

What is orange zest?
Orange zest is that orange colour of the orange peel grated either with the small sectioned side of a box grater or using an orange zester. Be careful to only grate the orange section of the peeling, avoiding the white part as the white part of the peel (the pith) is very bitter.

RECIPE HIGHLIGHTS
* Simple and Quick
* Low Glycemic
* Diabetic Friendly
* No Added Refined Sugars
* Vegetarian
* Vegan (if butter omitted)
* Dairy Free (if butter and yogurt omitted)
* High in Beta Carotene

☑ Nutritional Analysis

Amount Per Serving	
Calories	86.23
Total Fat	2.77 g
Saturated Fat	1.29 g
Cholesterol	3.82 mg
Sodium	150.66 mg
Potassium	408.34 mg
Total Carbohydrates	12.75 g
Fibre	2.91 g
Sugar	3.79 g
Protein	4.65 g

Creamy Cauliflower Soup

This soup is creamy without any added dairy. This is a great way to increase those hard to get vegetables during the winter months.

Serves 6

Ingredients

- 2 tablespoons of olive oil
- 2 cups of chopped onion
- 1 cup of diced carrots
- 1 cup of diced zucchini
- 1 cup of diced celery
- 8 cups of fresh or frozen cauliflower
- ½ cup of millet
- 8 cups of vegetable or chicken stock
- 2 cloves of garlic, crushed
- ½ teaspoon of sea salt
- Sea salt and pepper to taste

Directions

Heat oil in a large soup pot, add onions and sauté until soft.

Add the vegetables, millet, garlic and sea salt allowing to cook for 2 more minutes.

Add stock and bring to a boil.

Turn heat to medium and let simmer for 30-40 minutes or until vegetables are tender.

Using an immersion blender, purée soup until smooth and creamy. Serve piping hot.

Add sea salt and pepper to taste.

☑ Smart Facts

RECIPE HIGHLIGHTS

- * Dairy Free
- * Diabetic Friendly
- * Simple and Quick
- * No Added Refined Sugars
- * Low Glycemic
- * Vegetarian and Vegan

☑ Nutritional Analysis

Amount Per Serving

Calories	68.46
Total Fat	1.88 g
Saturated Fat	0.42 g
Cholesterol	0 mg
Sodium	100.39 mg
Potassium	463.21 mg
Total Carbohydrates	9.83 g
Fibre	2.69 g
Sugar	3.74 g
Protein	5.15 g

Creamy Fennel Soup

Fennel has a subtle almost 'licorice' like taste. The creaminess of this soup comes from the starch of the potato rather than actual cream making it a perfect soup for the dairy intolerant. *Serves 6*

Ingredients

- 1 tablespoon of olive oil or butter
- 1 fennel bulb chopped into bite size pieces (about 4 cups)
- 1½ cups of onions chopped
- 2 medium sized potatoes, peeled and chopped
- 5 cups of chicken or vegetable broth
- 1 teaspoon of sea salt
- 1 cup of coconut milk

Directions

In a large soup pot, on medium heat, add oil (or melt butter), chopped fennel, onion and potato. Cook gently until vegetables soften.

Add broth and bring mixture to a boil. Reduce heat to simmer and cook until vegetables are tender. Add coconut milk and sea salt and heat through.

Using an immersion blender, purée soup until creamy.

Garnish with the thin green wisps of the fennel leaf for a gourmet look.

☑ Smart Facts

Fennel is full of beneficial immune boosting nutrients including vitamin C, fibre, potassium, manganese, folate, niacin, phosphorous, calcium, magnesium, iron and copper.

RECIPE HIGHLIGHTS

- * Simple and Quick
- * Dairy Free
- * No Added Refined Sugars
- * Diabetic Friendly
- * Vegetarian and Vegan

☑ Nutritional Analysis

Amount Per Serving

Calories	160
Total Fat	8.7 g
Cholesterol	0 mg
Sodium	28.8 mg
Potassium	512.5 mg
Carbohydrates	15.8 g
Fibre	2.6 g
Sugar	1 g
Protein	2.4 g

Curried Butternut Squash and Apple Soup

This soup is absolutely amazing! Delicate in flavours and warming to the stomach.
Serves 12

Ingredients

- 2 cups of onions, chopped
- 2 tablespoons of butter or coconut oil if dairy intolerant
- 1 tablespoon of ground cumin
- 1 tablespoon of Garam Masala*
- 2 teaspoons of ground coriander
- 2 teaspoons of sea salt
- 6 cups of butternut squash, peeled and chopped
- 2 cups of sweet potatoes, peeled and coarsely chopped
- 2 cups of apples, peeled and coarsely chopped
- 6 cups of water or vegetable or chicken broth
- ½ cup of light coconut milk

Directions

In a large stock pot, sauté the onions and butter until the onions are soft and translucent.

Add the spices, squash, sweet potatoes, apples and cook a few minutes more. Add stock or water and coconut milk to the mixture.

Bring to a boil, then reduce heat and simmer for 30 minutes until the ingredients are soft and tender.

Purée the ingredients with an immersion blender.

Serve with a dollop of yogurt or swirl of coconut milk.

*Garam Masala is a blend of Indian spices. You can find this spice in health food stores, bulk food stores or Asian grocery stores.

☑ Smart Facts

RECIPE HIGHLIGHTS
* Dairy Free, if using coconut oil
* Low Glycemic
* Simple and Quick
* No Added Refined Sugars

☑ Nutritional Analysis

Amount Per Serving	
Calories	137.03
Total Fat	5.07 g
Saturated Fat	3.65 g
Cholesterol	6.11 mg
Sodium	275 mg
Potassium	492.67 mg
Total Carbohydrates	23.55 g
Fibre	3.52 g
Sugar	7.75 g
Protein	2.07 g

Butternut Squash and Banana Soup

This recipe is warming, rich and naturally sweet due to the roasted banana. Try this soup if you are looking for something different to warm you up. I love having this soup after a nice walk in the snow or a skate on the canal. *Serves 8*

Ingredients

- 5 cups of butternut squash peeled and cut into cubes
- 1 tablespoon of olive oil
- 1 tablespoon of honey
- 1 large, ripe unpeeled banana
- 1 tablespoon of butter or coconut oil
- 1 cup of onion, chopped
- 1 tablespoon of garlic, minced
- 1 teaspoon of curry
- ½ teaspoon of cinnamon
- ¼ teaspoon of nutmeg
- 3 cups of vegetable or chicken broth
- 1 cup of light or regular coconut milk
- Sea salt and pepper to taste

Directions

Preheat the oven to 375°F.

Toss the cubed butternut squash with the olive oil and honey in a large bowl.

Spread the squash out on a large baking pan. Place the unpeeled banana on a baking pan (or put beside the squash on the same pan).

Roast the squash and banana for 20 minutes. Remove the banana and continue roasting the squash for 10-12 minutes longer or until the squash has become tender.

Melt the butter/coconut oil in a large saucepan on medium heat. Add the chopped onions and cook for 5 minutes. Lower the heat and add garlic, curry, cinnamon and nutmeg.

☑ Smart Facts

Leaving the peeling on the banana allows the banana to retain its natural sweetness and allows it to roast in its own juices.

RECIPE HIGHLIGHTS

* Dairy Free , if using coconut oil
* Diabetic Friendly
* High in Vitamin A
* No Added Refined Sugars
* Low Glycemic
* Vegetarian (if using vegetable broth)

☑ Nutritional Analysis

Amount Per Serving	
Calories	151.71
Total Fat	7.92 g
Saturated Fat	4.72 g
Cholesterol	3.82 mg
Sodium	35.85 mg
Potassium	549.46 mg
Total Carbohydrates	20.76 g
Fibre	2.75 g
Sugar	7.17 g
Protein	3.8 g

Add roasted banana (remove the peel over the pan to save all the banana juices), squash, broth, and coconut milk to the onions and spices.

Bring entire mixture to a boil and then lower the heat and simmer for 5 minutes.

Purée with an immersion blender and add sea salt and pepper to taste.

Curried Pear and Parsnip Soup

This soup has a rich, luxurious flavour that is low in fat, with the complex flavours of parsnips, curry and pears married together. I can remember as a little girl my mother telling me that parsnips were "white carrots" as a way to get me to eat them. Well...it worked!

Serves 8

Ingredients

- 2 tablespoons of extra virgin olive oil or coconut oil
- 1 sweet onion, chopped
- 4 cups of parsnips, chopped
- 1 cup of peeled and chopped pears (I like Bartletts)
- 1 teaspoon of curry powder
- ¼ teaspoon of black pepper
- 4–4½ cups of chicken stock or vegan vegetable stock
- 1 bay leaf
- ¾ cup of regular or light coconut milk
- Sea salt to taste

Directions

Add olive oil to a large saucepan on medium heat. Add the onions and gently cook until translucent.

Add in the chopped parsnips and pears. Cook gently until they begin to soften, being careful not to brown the vegetables. Add curry powder and black pepper, stirring vegetables to coat. Add stock and bay leaf.

Reduce heat to low and bring soup to simmer. Simmer uncovered until vegetables and pears are soft, about 40 minutes.

Discard bay leaf and purée using an immersion blender until smooth. Return to saucepan, stir in coconut milk and heat through.

☑ Smart Facts

Europeans first brought the parsnip to North America in the early 1600's. This creamy-white root has become a North American favourite. The starch in the parsnips turns to a sugar after the first frost, giving parsnips a sweet, celery-like, nutty flavour.

RECIPE HIGHLIGHTS

* Simple and Quick
* Diabetic Friendly
* Low Glycemic
* No Added Refined Sugars
* Vegetarian and Vegan (if using vegetable broth)

☑ Nutritional Analysis

Amount Per Serving	
Calories	178.27
Total Fat	7.48 g
Saturated Fat	5.73 g
Cholesterol	0 mg
Sodium	68.03 mg
Potassium	625.03 mg
Total Carbohydrates	25.76 g
Fibre	5.76 g
Sugar	8.25 g
Protein	5.67 g

Season with sea salt to taste.

Homemade Chicken or Vegetable Soup Stock

The secret to a good soup is a homemade stock. The subtle flavours come from natural herbs, spices and vegetables as opposed to food additives, artificial flavours and food coloring found in store-bought soup stock.

Makes 8 cups

Ingredients

- Carcass of 1 chicken
- 2 whole carrots, scrubbed
- 3 whole cloves of garlic
- 2 celery stalks, including leaves, washed
- 2 whole onions, washed, cut in half with skins on
- 1 whole bay leaf
- 4 sprigs of fresh parsley
- Small bunch of fresh tarragon
- 1 teaspoon of dried Italian seasoning
- Juice of ½ lemon
- 1 teaspoon of black peppercorns
- Sea salt to taste
- 10 cups of cold water

Directions

Add chicken, carrots, garlic, celery, onions, bay leaf, herbs and peppercorn to a large soup pot. Cover with cold water. Cook uncovered until stock comes to a boil then reduce heat to a simmer.

Cook for a minimum of 4 hours or until about 8 cups of liquid remains.

Do not stir and do not allow stock to boil or it will become cloudy.

Strain through a fine sieve, discarding all solids.

Chill in refrigerator overnight and allow fat to congeal on the surface and remove.

Freeze in small batches.

To make the vegetable stock, follow the above directions, omitting the chicken.

☑ Smart Facts

Why do I add the juice of ½ of a lemon to my broth?
You add a squeeze of lemon to your broth as the acidity of the lemon will leach out calcium from the chicken bones making this soup stock a bone building broth. Homemade broth is loaded with vitamins and minerals.

RECIPE HIGHLIGHTS
* Dairy Free
* Simple and Quick
* No Added Refined Sugars
* Low Glycemic
* Diabetic Friendly

☑ Nutritional Analysis

Fat and calories are minimal.

Homemade Vegan Soup Stock

The secret to a good soup is a homemade stock. And you can control the salt! Enjoy this vegan version of my homemade soup stock.

Makes 8 cups

Ingredients

- 3 whole carrots, scrubbed
- 6 whole cloves of garlic
- 4 celery stalks, including leaves, washed
- 4 whole onions, washed, cut in half with skins on
- 1 whole bay leaf
- 4 sprigs of fresh parsley
- 1 teaspoon of Italian seasoning
- 1 teaspoon of black peppercorns
- Sea salt to taste
- 12 cups of cold water

Directions

Add carrots, garlic, celery, onions, bay leaf, herbs and peppercorn to a large soup pot. Cover with cold water. Cook uncovered until stock comes to a boil, then turn heat down to simmer.

Cook for a minimum of 4 hours or until about 8 cups of liquid remains.

Do not stir and do not allow stock to boil or it will become cloudy.

Strain through a fine sieve, discarding all solids.

Chill liquid and store in refrigerator overnight and freeze in small batches.

☑ Smart Facts

Why do I keep the peeling on the onions?
Leaving the peeling on the onions gives your broth a beautiful golden color that comes from the natural pigment of the onion skin.

RECIPE HIGHLIGHTS
* Dairy Free
* Simple and Quick
* No Added Refined Sugars
* Low Glycemic
* Diabetic Friendly
* Vegetarian and Vegan

☑ Nutritional Analysis

Fat and calories are minimal.

Roasted Asparagus Soup

This is an absolutely delicious soup that is perfect to make during the springtime when asparagus is the most plentiful. One of my favorite things about spring happens when our local asparagus farm puts their sign out that says 'fresh asparagus' is available. Asparagus is a sure sign of spring in Ontario. *Serves 8*

Ingredients

- 3 pounds of asparagus, ends trimmed
- 2 cloves of garlic, peeled and chopped fine
- 1 medium onion, diced
- 4 cups of chicken or vegetable broth
- 2 tablespoons of ground almonds or unsweetened almond butter
- Sea salt and pepper to taste

Directions

Preheat oven to 425°F.

Place the asparagus spears on a large baking sheet, spread out in a single layer. Roast for 10 minutes. Turn asparagus over and sprinkle the onion and garlic on top. Roast for 10 more minutes or until tender. Remove roasted asparagus, onions and garlic from the oven and cut asparagus into pieces, reserving 8 asparagus tops for garnish later.

In a medium sauce pan, add chopped asparagus, garlic and onions. Add ground almonds or almond butter and pour in broth. Bring to a boil on medium high heat then reduce heat to low and simmer soup for 10 minutes. Add sea salt and pepper to taste.

Purée soup with immersion blender, pour into bowls and garnish each bowl with reserved asparagus spear.

☑ Smart Facts

What is almond butter and where can I find it?
Almond butter contains no butter at all contrary to its name. Almond butter consists of almonds ground into nut butter. It is similar to peanut butter only almond butter has a milder, more elegant taste. Almond butter is an excellent source of vitamin E, protein and heart healthy mono-saturated fat.

RECIPE HIGHLIGHTS

* Simple and Quick
* Dairy Free
* No Added Refined Sugars
* Diabetic Friendly
* Low Glycemic
* Vegetarian and Vegan (if using vegetable broth)

☑ Nutritional Analysis

Amount Per Serving

Calories	73.32
Total Fat	2.08 g
Saturated Fat	0.38 g
Cholesterol	0 mg
Sodium	40.16 mg
Potassium	488.21 mg
Total Carbohydrates	10.13 g
Fibre	4.1 g
Sugar	4.11 g
Protein	6.83 g

Spicy Black Bean Chili

This chili is a Southwestern-style, nutrient dense dish that is chockful of vegetables, fibre and protein. I love to serve this on a baked potato topped with chopped fresh cilantro, green onions and Greek yogurt. *Serves 6*

Ingredients

- 1 tablespoon of olive oil
- ½ large Spanish onion, chopped fine
- 2 cloves of garlic, chopped
- 1 diced green pepper
- 1 (15-ounce) can of drained black beans
- ½ cup frozen, fresh or canned corn kernels
- 2 tablespoons each of cumin, chili powder and Italian seasoning
- 1 cup of chicken or vegetable broth
- 1 (12-ounce/355-milliliter) can of V8 juice
- ½ teaspoon each of sea salt and pepper
- ¼ cup of fresh cilantro, chopped

Directions

In a medium sauce pan, heat olive oil and add the onion, garlic and green pepper. Gently cook the vegetables until tender. Add the beans, corn and spices and cook gently allowing the spices to infuse with the beans. Add stock and V8 juice and bring mixture to simmer for 15 minutes.

Remove from heat, season with sea salt and pepper. Mix in chopped cilantro and serve hot with gluten-free buns, baked potato or warm corn tortillas.

☑ Smart Facts

Black beans are extremely high in fibre and protein. A one cup serving gives you 12 grams of fibre and 14 grams of protein!

RECIPE HIGHLIGHTS
* Dairy Free
* High in Fibre
* High in Protein
* No Added Refined Sugar
* Vegetarian and Vegan

☑ Nutritional Analysis

Amount Per Serving	
Calories	172.92
Total Fat	3.99 g
Saturated Fat	0.61 g
Cholesterol	0 mg
Sodium	225.39 mg
Potassium	593.14 mg
Total Carbohydrates	27.99 g
Fibre	8.94 g
Sugar	3.82 g
Protein	9.13 g

Smokey Red Pepper Soup

The smokiness of the roasted red pepper blends together with the aromatic undertone of onion and rosemary to create a smooth soup without the added fat from cream. I love to serve this in a white bowl topped with a sprig of fresh rosemary picked from my herb garden.

Serves 4

Ingredients

- 4 sweet red peppers, whole
- 2 tablespoons of butter or coconut oil if dairy intolerant/vegan
- 1 cup of finely chopped onion
- 1 teaspoon of dried rosemary or one tablespoon fresh
- 5 cups of chicken or vegetable stock
- 3 tablespoons of tomato paste
- 1 teaspoon of sea salt
- 4 teaspoons of coconut milk

Directions

Preheat oven to broil. Put whole red peppers on baking sheet under broiler and turn regularly until the skins have blackened. Remove peppers from oven and place into sealed plastic bag and let stand for 20 minutes.

Peel off skin from peppers and remove seeds and stem. Halve peppers while trying to save any juices that run out. Set aside.

Melt butter/coconut oil in a saucepan and add onion and rosemary, cooking gently over low heat for 5 minutes. Add peppers with juices and stock and bring to a boil. Reduce heat and simmer for 15 minutes. Add tomato paste and sea salt.

Remove from heat and purée with an immersion blender until smooth. Strain soup through a fine strainer and reheat in saucepan.

Red peppers are low in calories and high in vitamin C, which helps to fight infections, heart disease and cancer. Other key nutrients found in this colourful vegetable include calcium, iron, magnesium, phosphorus, zinc and B vitamins just to name a few.

RECIPE HIGHLIGHTS

* Dairy free
* Vegetarian
* Vegan
* Low Glycemic
* Diabetic Friendly
* High in Vitamin C

☑ Nutritional Analysis

Amount Per Serving	
Calories	107.14
Total Fat	5.38 g
Saturated Fat	2.83 g
Cholesterol	10.18 mg
Sodium	200.36 mg
Potassium	435.47 mg
Total Carbohydrates	10.78 g
Fibre	2.52 g
Sugar	5.52 g
Protein	5.36 g

Serve soup hot or chilled and garnish with pepper, paprika and a delicate swirl of coconut milk on top.

Thai Inspired Vegan Stew

I made this stew on a snowy winter day and just fell in love with it. It is a warming stew with just the right amount of heat from the curry paste and sweet from the coconut milk. This stew is also chockful of vegetables and legumes making it very hearty without any meat.

Serves 6

Ingredients

- 1 tablespoon of coconut oil or olive oil
- 1 medium onion, chopped
- 2 tablespoons each of minced garlic and chopped fresh ginger
- 3 tablespoons of Thai red curry paste
- ¼ cup of unsweetened peanut butter or almond butter
- 4 cups of diced mixture of carrots, sweet potatoes and potatoes
- 1 (19-ounce/540-millilitre) can of chickpeas, drained
- 1 (9-ounce/280-millilitre) can of peas, drained
- 2 tablespoons of golden raisins
- 2 cups of vegetable broth
- 1 (9-ounce/280-millilitre) can of coconut milk
- 4 cups of baby spinach or chopped Swiss chard
- Sea salt and pepper to taste

Directions

Heat coconut oil in medium saucepan. Add the onions and cook gently until golden brown. Add garlic and ginger and stir constantly for 1 minute. Add curry paste and nut butter and stir until well combined. Add vegetables, chickpeas, peas and raisins stirring well and allowing the vegetables to infuse with the flavours of the onions and curry paste. Cook for 5 minutes while mixing well.

Add the broth and bring mixture to a simmer.

Coconut milk is derived from the flesh of the coconut. Coconut milk does not contain any dairy and the main saturated fat that it contains, lauric acid, is also found in mother's milk and has been shown to promote brain development and bone health.

RECIPE HIGHLIGHTS

* Dairy Free
* No Added Refined Sugars
* Diabetic Friendly
* Low Glycemic
* Vegetarian and Vegan
* High in Iron

☑ Nutritional Analysis

Amount Per Serving

Calories	317.57
Saturated Fat	10.32 g
Cholesterol	0 mg
Sodium	300 mg
Potassium	803.75 mg
Total Carbohydrates	37.37 g
Fibre	7.07 g
Sugar	8.97 g
Protein	9.2 g

Let cook until the vegetables are tender, about 20 minutes. Add coconut milk and heat through.

Just before serving, add in baby spinach or chard and allow it to wilt, cooking for about 1 minute longer. Serve stew piping hot.

Creamy Broccoli Soup

Ingredients

- 1 tablespoon of olive oil or coconut oil
- 2 onions, chopped
- 2 potatoes, peeled and coarsely chopped
- 2 cups vegetable stock
- 1 teaspoon of sea salt and pepper
- 3.5 cups of fresh or frozen broccoli pieces
- 1 cup of unsweetened almond milk

Directions

In large saucepan, heat oil over medium heat; cook onions and potatoes, stirring often, until onions are softened, about 10 minutes. Add stock, salt and pepper; bring to boil. Reduce heat to medium; cover and simmer until potatoes are tender, about 15 minutes. Add broccoli pieces and almond milk; cover and cook for 5 minutes.

Puree with an immersion blender.

☑ Smart Facts

RECIPE HIGHLIGHTS
* Dairy Free
* No Added Refined Sugars
* Diabetic Friendly
* Vegetarian and Vegan

☑ Nutritional Analysis

Amount Per Serving	
Calories	75.19
Total Fat	2.27g
Saturated Fat	0.3g
Cholesterol	0mg
Sodium	171.71mg
Potassium	383.37mg
Total Carbohydrates	12.9g
Fiber	1.21g
Sugar	1.8g
Protein	2.17g

Fresh, Moist and Chewy Gluten-Free Bread

I really cannot imagine life without bread! This bread is soft, hearty and so delicious when it comes fresh out of the bread maker. Enjoy this bread as much as I have creating it!

Serves 12-18

Ingredients

- 3 whole eggs
- 1 tablespoon of apple cider vinegar
- ¼ cup of melted butter or coconut oil
- ¼ cup of honey
- 1½ cups of buttermilk at room temperature (if dairy intolerant use 1 cup of almond milk and ⅓ cup of ground almonds)
- 1 teaspoon of sea salt
- 1 tablespoon of xanthan gum
- ⅓ cup of tapioca starch
- ½ cup of both potato starch and sorghum flour
- 2 cups of brown rice flour
- 1 tablespoon of dry active yeast
- 2 tablespoons of both sesame seeds and whole quinoa

Directions

Pre-grease 1½ pound loaf pan with butter or coconut oil.

Place all ingredients into a bread machine in the order recommended by the manufacturer

Select the fast cycle on the bread machine. Add a splash of buttermilk if more liquid is required.

Let bread cool for 10-15 minutes before removing from pan.

☑ Smart Facts

Sorghum is among the most harvested cereal products in the world. It is one of the oldest known grains and is a major human food source in Africa and India.

Sorghum is very high in fibre and iron, with a fairly high protein level as well making it an excellent choice for both the taste and the health benefits.

You can find sorghum flour at your local health food store.

RECIPE HIGHLIGHTS
- Easy to Make
- Good Source of Protein
- Low Glycemic
- No Added Refined Sugars
- Diabetic Friendly

☑ Nutritional Analysis

Amount Per Serving	
Calories	172.28
Total Fat	4.5 g
Saturated Fat	2 g
Cholesterol	42.85 mg
Sodium	160.85 mg
Potassium	174.14 mg
Total Carbohydrates	28.18 g
Fibre	2 g
Sugar	5.26 g
Protein	5 g

Main Courses

One of the most important memory builders is to sit down with friends and family to share, laugh and talk over a meal. Enjoy these memory makers and know that each and every one has been shared with my family and friends.

List of recipes:

- Brown Lentil Curry
- Channa Masala "Chickpea Curry"
- Colourful Salmon Skewers for the BBQ
- Coriander and Ginger Marinated Lamb
- Earthy Salsa Chicken
- Fillet of Sole Almandine
- Gluten-Free Lasagne
- Grilled Chicken or Beef Fajitas
- Halibut with Caramelized Onions
- Honey Baked Curry Chicken
- Jamaican Jerk Chicken
- Lamb burgers
- Mediterranean-Style Salmon
- Old Fashioned Fall Stew
- Roasted Pecan Crusted Fish Sticks
- Slowly Simmered Beef Fajitas

- Turkey Burgers
- Fillet of Sole Almandine
- Brads Burkey Burgers
- Gluten-Free Tourtière
- Lemon Dill Chicken
- Cauliflower Crust Pizza
- Maple Grilled Salmon
- Spicy Curry Chicken
  with Creamy Peanut Sauce

Brown Lentil Curry

This recipe comes from my friend and colleague Sabha. She first brought me this yummy curry for lunch one day and I just had to have this recipe.

I first met Sabha in a health food store many years ago. We became fast friends and Sabha is not only a wonderful friend and colleague but a marvelous cook. *Serves 8*

Ingredients

- 2 cups of brown lentils
- Water for soaking
- 8 cups of water
- 2 medium onions, chopped
- 4 cloves of garlic, chopped
- 2 teaspoons of sea salt
- 2 tablespoons of curry powder
- 3/4 cup of crushed, canned tomatoes or 3 tablespoons of tomato paste
- 1 tablespoon of ground coriander
- 1 teaspoon of garam masala
- 1 teaspoon of onion seeds (these are little black seeds found in Asian Grocery Stores)
- 1/4 cup of olive oil or coconut oil

Directions

Soak the lentils in a bowl of 6 cups of water for about 1½ hours. The lentils will absorb a lot of the liquid. Drain the remaining liquid.

Place 8 cups of water in a large pot and place on stove over high heat. Add soaked lentils, onions, garlic, sea salt and curry powder to the water. Bring to a boil and reduce to medium-low heat to simmer. Cover pot and cook for approximately ½ hour. Add tomatoes or tomato paste and continue to cook on medium-low heat for another ½ hour until lentils are tender. Add the garam masala and ground coriander. Continue cooking lentils uncovered until slightly thickened (about 15-20 minutes), stirring occasionally.

☑ Smart Facts

Black onion seeds contain 15 amino acids and 84 fatty acids containing compounds that are antifungal and antiviral. They have been known to increase immune enhancing T-cells, reduce inflammation and detoxify the liver.

You can find black onion seeds at most Asian grocery stores.

RECIPE HIGHLIGHTS

* Simple and Quick
* Dairy Free
* No Added Refined Sugars
* Low Glycemic
* Diabetic Friendly
* Vegetarian and Vegan
* High in Protein and Fibre

☑ Nutritional Analysis

Amount Per Serving	
Calories	259
Saturated Fat	0.64 g
Cholesterol	0 mg
Sodium	308 mg
Potassium	606.81 mg
Total Carbohydrates	35.17 g
Fibre	16.41 g
Sugar	2.33 g
Protein	13.47 g

Heat olive oil/coconut oil in a small pot on medium heat and fry the onion seeds until they start to sizzle—be careful not to burn them—then add oil and onion seeds to the cooked curry and stir well.

Channa Masala "Chickpea Curry"

This recipe was first introduced to me by a friend who grew up in India. This is a recipe that has not only enriched our palettes but enriched our lives. Good recipes are like that, they become like an old friend. This recipe is that old friend for us— reliable, trustworthy and just plain wonderful to have around! *Serves 12*

Ingredients

- ¼ cup of coconut oil or olive oil
- 2 cups of cooking onions, diced
- 1 tablespoon of Jeera (Sah Jeeru) or cumin seeds
- 2 tablespoons of peeled garlic, chopped
- 3 tablespoons of fresh, peeled, grated, ginger root
- 1 tablespoon each of ground cumin, ground coriander, turmeric and Garam Masala*
- ½ teaspoon of cayenne pepper
- 1½ teaspoons of sea salt
- ½ tablespoon of ground black pepper
- 1 (5-ounce/156-millilitre) small can of tomato paste
- 1 (23-ounce/680-millilitre) can of crushed tomatoes
- 2 (19-ounce) cans of chickpeas, drained and rinsed
- 1 cup of plain 2% yogurt or coconut milk
- 1 teaspoon of fresh lime juice

Optional Add In:
- 1 cup of frozen peas or 1 cup of cooked, diced chicken thighs/chicken breasts

Directions

Sauté onions on low heat in oil until they start to brown. Add Jeera and cook on low heat for 1 minute, constantly stirring. Add garlic and ginger and continue to cook on low heat until the ginger root begins to stick to the bottom. Add the spices and cook on low heat until the flavours have blended. Add the tomatoes,

chickpeas, yogurt, lime juice and add the optional peas and chicken. Continue to cook gently until sauce thickens.

Serve with brown rice or quinoa and garnish with fresh, chopped cilantro.

This spice can be found in an Asian or Indian grocery store.

☑ Smart Facts

Chickpeas, also known as garbanzo beans are known for their delicious nut like taste, high protein and fibre content. Chickpeas are one of the oldest legumes to be cultivated by humans.

RECIPE HIGHLIGHTS

* Simple and Quick
* High in Fibre
* Low Glycemic
* Vegetarian and Vegan (if using coconut milk)

☑ Nutritional Analysis

Amount Per Serving

Calories	146
Total Fat	5.6 g
Saturated Fat	.92 g
Cholesterol	1.2 mg
Sodium	280 mg
Potassium	333.6 mg
Carbohydrates	20.2 g
Fibre	3.7 g
Sugar	4.3 g
Protein	5 g

Coriander and Ginger Marinated Lamb

This is a quick and easy marinade that tastes great. If you especially enjoy sauces, double the recipe and simmer the leftovers for a sauce to serve with the meat. This marinade works just as well for chicken. Enjoy! *Serves 6-8*

Ingredients

- 1 leg of lamb (3 pounds), boneless and tied

  Marinade:
- 2 teaspoons of dried coriander
- 1 cup of fresh lemon juice
- 4 teaspoons of extra virgin olive oil
- 1 large Spanish onion, finely chopped
- 2 tablespoons of fresh grated ginger
- 4 cloves of fresh garlic, crushed
- 2 teaspoons of ground black pepper

Directions

Combine ingredients for the marinade into a bowl and whisk until well mixed. Coat the lamb and let marinate overnight in the refrigerator.

Preheat oven to 425°F or set BBQ to high.

BBQ or roast the lamb to desired doneness. Allow to stand for 15 minutes (covered) before carving.

☑ Smart Facts

RECIPE HIGHLIGHTS
* Dairy Free
* Low Glycemic
* No Added Refined Sugars
* Diabetic Friendly
* High in Protein
* High in Iron

☑ Nutritional Analysis

Amount Per Serving	
Calories	379.83
Saturated Fat	10.19 g
Cholesterol	113.97 mg
Sodium	98.71 mg
Potassium	507.35 mg
Total Carbohydrates	5 g
Fibre	0.58 g
Sugar	0.79 g
Protein	32.09 g

Colourful Salmon Skewers for the BBQ

These kebabs came about over a May long weekend when my 5 year old niece and I were cooking together. I typically find salmon too strong a flavour for me; however, by adding the onions and the peppers the flavour is mellowed, appealing to even the most critical taste buds. These skewers are simple enough for even a 5 year old to make and are even pretty to look at!
Serves 4

Ingredients

- 6 ounces of wild salmon fillets cut into bite size pieces
- ½ cup each of green, yellow and red pepper, cut into bite size pieces
- 1 medium red onion, cut into bite size pieces
- Cracked black pepper to taste
- 4 large or 6 small wooden skewers
- Olive oil for grill

Directions

Soak wooden skewers in water for several hours before preparing them.

Preheat BBQ to medium.

Take the wooden skewers and spear a piece of red onion pushing it to the bottom of the skewer. Add a piece of salmon and push it down to meet the onion, then add a piece of pepper and keep layering vegetables and fish until the skewers are full.

Sprinkle each skewer with cracked black pepper.

Brush the BBQ with olive oil and grill skewers until the salmon is cooked and the vegetables are crisp/tender (about 6-10 minutes).

☑ Smart Facts

Salmon is one of nature's best sources of Omega 3 fatty acids. Omega 3 fatty acids help decrease the risk of heart disease and high cholesterol at the same time as increasing memory capacity. They also help maintain healthy skin, hair and nails while reducing wrinkles.

RECIPE HIGHLIGHTS

* Simple and Quick
* Dairy Free
* Low Glycemic
* No Added Refined Sugars
* Diabetic Friendly
* High in Protein
* High in Omega 3 Fats

☑ Nutritional Analysis

Amount Per Serving

Calories	88.17
Saturated Fat	0.45 g
Cholesterol	23.38 mg
Sodium	21.4 mg
Potassium	316.73 mg
Total Carbohydrates	6.18 g
Fibre	1.49 g
Sugar	1.2 g
Protein	9.36 g

Earthy Salsa Chicken

This is one of the easiest recipes to make, yet it is always a surprise to people how tasty and tender the chicken pieces are. *Serves 2*

Ingredients

- 8 ounces boneless, skinless chicken breast, cut into cubes
- 1 cup of homemade or purchased salsa
- ½ teaspoon of ground cumin

Directions

Preheat oven to 350°F.

Combine the chicken, salsa and cumin in a small bowl and mix thoroughly. Add to a casserole dish and bake in the oven, covered for 35-40 minutes.

Fill a gluten-free wrap with chicken, lettuce, avocado and salsa and serve. This dish is also excellent over rice or with gluten-free pasta noodles.

☑ Smart Facts

Did you know? Cumin is very rich in iron (above 66 mg in each 100 g) which is more than 5 times the daily requirement of iron for an adult. Cumin also has a considerable amount of vitamin-C, which is essential for a good immune system, iron absorption and keeping infections away. Cumin can be a nutritious additive to the daily diet of lactating mothers, women in their menses or anemic individuals.

RECIPE HIGHLIGHTS

* Simple and Quick
* Dairy Free
* Diabetic Friendly
* High Protein
* Low Glycemic
* No Added Refined Sugar

☑ Nutritional Analysis

Amount Per Serving	
Calories	224.04
Saturated Fat	1.19 g
Cholesterol	96.39 mg
Sodium	286 mg
Potassium	684.31 mg
Total Carbohydrates	8.34 g
Fibre	2.13 g
Sugar	3.97 g
Protein	37.26 g

Fillet of Sole Almandine

This dish is a great compliment for the ratatouille and the roasted baby bok choy making a complete meal that is simple and nutritious.

Serves 4

Ingredients

- 4 4-ounce fillets of fresh sole
- 2 tablespoons of olive oil
- ½ cup of toasted, slivered almonds
- Sea salt and pepper to taste
- Juice of ½ lemon

Directions

Preheat oven to 350°F.

Rinse fish with cold water and pat dry. Brush fillets lightly with olive oil. Place fish in parchment-lined baking dish, sprinkle with almonds. Squeeze lemon juice on the fillets.

Bake for 12 minutes or until fish is flakey when pricked with a fork. Season to taste with salt and pepper.

This is excellent with brown rice pilaf and sautéed vegetables.

☑ Smart Facts

The *Journal of the American Medical Association* reported a study by Brigham and Women's Hospital that eating at least 1 meal of fish weekly can cut the risk of sudden cardiac death in men in half! Fish is clearly a healthy addition to any diet.

RECIPE HIGHLIGHTS

* Egg Free
* Simple and Quick
* Dairy Free
* Low Glycemic
* No Added Refined Sugars
* Diabetic Friendly

☑ Nutritional Analysis

Amount Per Serving

Calories	265.5
Total Fat	14.22 g
Saturated Fat	1.58 g
Cholesterol	77.11 mg
Sodium	119.31 mg
Potassium	518.81 mg
Total Carbohydrates	3.33 g
Fibre	2.04 g
Sugar	0.85 g
Protein	31.21 g

Grilled Chicken or Beef Fajitas

This is always a crowd pleaser and a fail-safe when you're entertaining. It's easy to prepare ahead of time and everyone loves to assemble their own. *Serves 6*

Ingredients

- 18 ounces beef flank steak, top sirloin or chicken breast
- 1 large onion, chopped
- 1 large green and red bell pepper, sliced
- 3 cloves of garlic, minced
- 2 tablespoons of chili powder
- 2 tablespoons of ground coriander
- 2 teaspoons of red pepper flakes (adjust to taste)
- 1 tablespoon of olive oil
- Juice of 3 limes
- A tiny pinch of cinnamon
- Your choice of gluten-free tortilla wrap

Directions

Combine chili powder, coriander, red pepper flakes, cinnamon, minced garlic, olive oil and lime juice for marinade. Coat meat and marinate overnight.

Grill the meat on medium-high heat to desired doneness, ensuring chicken is well cooked.

Sautee the onion and bell pepper in a cast iron frying pan to desired firmness. Slice the meat across the grain and lay atop the onions and peppers.

Serve the pan directly to the table and enjoy the sizzle. Serve with a selection of lettuce, salsa, Greek yogurt, avocado or guacamole, cheddar cheese, fresh cilantro or anything else you would like to pile on.

☑ Smart Facts

Gluten free tortillas are available in the health food section of most grocery stores or at your local health food store.

Note: Nutritional Analysis varies with condiments.

RECIPE HIGHLIGHTS

* Simple and Quick
* Dairy Free
* No Added Refined Sugars
* High in Protein and Iron
* Diabetic Friendly
* Low Glycemic

☑ Nutritional Analysis

Amount Per Serving	
Calories	117
Total Fat	1.2 g
Saturated Fat	0.3 g
Cholesterol	49.3 mg
Sodium	58 mg
Potassium	348.7 mg
Carbohydrates	4.8 g
Fibre	1.4 g
Sugar	2.9 g
Protein	20.3 g

Gluten-Free Lasagna

My husband confidently declared one day while on holidays that, "Our diet does not have enough lasagna in it." Spoken like a true 100% meat and potatoes kind of guy, my goal was to find a gluten-free recipe he would enjoy. According to Brad, this recipe is Garfield approved! *Serves 8*

Ingredients

- 2 cups of cottage cheese
- 1 egg, beaten
- 1 package of Rizopia gluten-free 'oven ready' lasagne noodles
- 4 cups of your favourite meat or vegetable spaghetti sauce
- 1 cup of sliced mushrooms
- 1 package of frozen spinach (454 grams), chopped
- 1 cup of Mozzarella cheese, grated

Directions

Preheat oven to 350°F.

Drain the cottage cheese in a colander to remove all excess water. Place the strained cottage cheese in a bowl and blend in the egg. Set aside.

Cover the bottom of a 9 by 13 inch casserole dish with 1 cup of sauce. Place lasagna noodles on top of the sauce, lining the bottom of the dish. Add 1 cup of the cottage cheese-egg mixture to cover the noodles. Add ½ package of spinach and ½ cup of sliced mushrooms to cover all of the cottage cheese mixture.

Add 3-4 more lasagne noodles and continue layering until reaching the top of dish. Top the lasagna off with grated Mozzarella cheese.

☑ Smart Facts

I will often add ½ can of low sodium V8 juice to my tomato sauces instead of adding water and tomato paste. It is an easy way to sneak vegetables into a dish like lasagna or chili!

RECIPE HIGHLIGHTS

* Simple and Quick
* Low Glycemic
* Diabetic Friendly
* No added Refined Sugars
* High in Iron

☑ Nutritional Analysis

Amount Per Serving

Calories	156.95
Total Fat	5.23 g
Saturated Fat	2.1 g
Cholesterol	31.05 mg
Sodium	450 mg
Potassium	436.22 mg
Total Carbohydrates	16.45 g
Fibre	2.87 g
Sugar	9.49 g
Protein	10.66 g

Cover with foil and bake in the oven for 45 minutes. Remove the foil and continue to cook for another 10 minutes until the cheese is brown and bubbling. Let stand for 10 minutes before serving.

Halibut with Caramelized Onions

I just love caramelized onions! Sometimes I caramelize onions just before Brad comes home so he can be welcomed by the smell of a home cooked meal. *Serves 4*

Ingredients

- 1 tablespoon of butter, coconut oil or olive oil
- 1 large Spanish/yellow onion sliced thin
- 1 tablespoon of maple syrup
- 1 teaspoon of balsamic vinegar
- 16 ounces of halibut fillet cut into 4-ounce portions
- 1 tablespoon of butter (melted), coconut oil or olive oil
- Sea salt and pepper to taste

Directions

Preheat broiler to 475°F.

Heat the butter/oil over medium heat in a large skillet. Add the onions, stir well and reduce heat to low. Cook for 15-20 minutes stirring occasionally until onions are soft and golden brown.

Add the maple syrup and vinegar to onions and cook for 2 minutes, stirring constantly.

Brush melted butter over fish fillets. Place on parchment-lined baking sheet and sear under the broiler for 5 minutes. Turn fish, then reduce heat and cook for 10 minutes. Remove fish from the oven and season to taste with sea salt and pepper.

Top with caramelized onions.

☑ Smart Facts

Fish is an excellent source of muscle building protein providing 30 grams per 4-ounce serving!

RECIPE HIGHLIGHTS

* Simple and Quick
* Egg Free
* High in Protein
* Low Glycemic
* No Added Refined Sugar
* Diabetic Friendly

☑ Nutritional Analysis

Amount Per Serving	
Calories	244.87
Total Fat	10.12 g
Saturated Fat	1.42 g
Cholesterol	46.49 mg
Sodium	80.36 mg
Potassium	709.56 mg
Total Carbohydrates	6.43 g
Fibre	0.52 g
Sugar	4.47 g
Protein	30.61 g

Jamaican Jerk Chicken

Contrasting flavours can be bliss. The unique combination of allspice, cinnamon, nutmeg and the heat of red pepper flakes contrasts wonderfully with the sweetness of honey and BBQ to create a recipe you will enjoy over and over.

My brother-in-law Brian would rave to me about his amazing jerk chicken so much that I just had to try it. One fall day at the cottage I found his recipe on a scrap piece of paper in the 'family cottage cookbook'. I added a few of my own tweaks and have to admit, this is an AMAZING jerk chicken recipe. *Serves 4*

Ingredients

- 8 boneless, skinless chicken thighs (approximately 16 ounces)
- 1 cup of red onion, chopped
- 2 teaspoons each of ground thyme and honey
- 1 teaspoon of sea salt
- ½ teaspoon each of allspice, cinnamon and ground nutmeg
- 1 teaspoon each of red pepper flakes and black pepper
- 2 tablespoons of gluten-free Tamari sauce or Braggs Amino Acids
- 1 tablespoon each of olive oil, white vinegar and fresh lime juice
- 4 tablespoons of your favourite gluten-free BBQ sauce

Directions

Place all ingredients except BBQ sauce and chicken into a food processor or blender and blend well. Put chicken thighs and puréed sauce in a large Ziploc bag, toss to coat and let marinate in the fridge for a minimum of 1 hour, the longer the better (can be marinated overnight).

Preheat BBQ grill to medium.

Remove chicken from the jerk sauce and discard extra sauce.

Place chicken on grill and brush with BBQ sauce on each side (about ½ tablespoon of BBQ sauce per thigh). Grill chicken for 7 minutes on each side or until juices run clear when thigh is pierced with a fork. In the last minute of cooking, brush each thigh with extra BBQ sauce.

☑ Smart Facts

Jerk is the process of spicing and grilling meats, poultry and even vegetables, although the most popular are jerk pork and jerk chicken. The resulting food yields a spicy-sweet flavour and tender texture.

RECIPE HIGHLIGHTS

* Dairy Free
* Low Glycemic
* High in protein
* Diabetic Friendly

☑ Nutritional Analysis

Amount Per Serving

Calories	237
Total Fat	9.4 g
Saturated Fat	1.99 g
Cholesterol	125.5 mg
Sodium	219.1 mg
Potassium	424 mg
Carbohydrates	6.6 g
Fibre	<1 g
Sugar	3.7 g
Protein	30.2 g

Honey Baked Curry Chicken

This recipe is so simple and was a childhood favourite of mine. There is just a hint of curry that is complimented nicely by the honey glaze. It was one of those smells that brought a smile to my face when I stepped through the door after walking home from school. *Serves 4*

Ingredients

- 4 4-ounce boneless, skinless chicken breasts
- 2 tablespoons of butter
- 2 tablespoons of liquid honey
- 1 teaspoon of curry powder
- A pinch of sea salt

Directions

Preheat oven to 350°F.

Combine all of the above ingredients, excluding the chicken, in a small saucepan and heat on low heat until butter has melted.

Place chicken breasts in a lightly greased casserole dish. Pour the sauce over the chicken and cook covered for 35–45 minutes.

☑ Smart Facts

What is curry powder? Curry powder is a mixture of many herbs and spices. The combination of spices used in making curry powder varies between countries and regions, but the one ingredient that is present in all mixtures is 'turmeric'. Curcumin is the substance that gives turmeric its yellow color and is responsible for many of the health benefits derived from curry. Curcumin is a powerful antioxidant and anti-inflammatory agent, helping to reduce inflammation in the joints.

RECIPE HIGHLIGHTS

* Simple and Quick
* High in protein
* Low Glycemic
* Diabetic Friendly
* No Added Refined Sugars

☑ Nutritional Analysis

Amount Per Serving	
Calories	214.06
Total Fat	10.82 g
Saturated Fat	5.74 g
Cholesterol	93.45 mg
Sodium	118.46 mg
Potassium	230.6 mg
Total Carbohydrates	1.02 g
Fibre	0.17 g
Sugar	0.74 g
Protein	26.82 g

Lamb Burgers

This lamb is perfectly spiced with cumin, fresh mint and for a bit of heat, cayenne; which makes for a refreshing change from regular hamburgers. *Serves 4*

Ingredients

- 1 pound of ground lamb
- 1 onion, diced
- 1 clove of garlic, crushed
- 1 teaspoon of cumin
- 1 teaspoon of cayenne
- 2 tablespoons of fresh mint, chopped
- 2 tablespoons of fresh parsley, chopped
- 1 egg, beaten
- ¼ cup of gluten-free oatmeal
- ½ teaspoon each of sea salt and pepper

Directions

Preheat BBQ to medium.

Combine all above ingredients in a medium bowl, mixing thoroughly. Form mixture into patties 1-inch thick and grill on the BBQ until thoroughly cooked.

Serve in a gluten-free pita or on a gluten-free bun with hummus, lettuce and tomatoes.

☑ Smart Facts

RECIPE HIGHLIGHTS
* Simple and Quick
* No Added Refined Sugars
* High in Protein
* High in Iron

☑ Nutritional Analysis

Amount Per Serving

Calories	184.35
Calories From Fat	103.36
Total Fat	11.48 g
Saturated Fat	4.56 g
Cholesterol	85.85 mg
Sodium	213.22 mg
Potassium	256.25 mg
Total Carbohydrates	5 g
Fibre	0.92 g
Sugar	1.03 g
Protein	14.85 g

Mediterranean-Style Salmon

Enjoy this dish with a side of greens and brown rice for a truly healthy and satisfying meal.
Serves 4

Ingredients

- 2 tablespoons of extra virgin olive oil
- 1 tablespoon of fresh lemon juice
- 1 tablespoon of fresh lime juice
- 1 tablespoon of garlic, minced
- ¾ tablespoon of dried oregano
- 1 cup of cherry tomatoes cut in half
- 2 shallots or white parts of green onions, diced
- ⅓ cup of black or green olives, pitted and sliced
- 4 salmon fillets (about 6 ounces each)

Directions

Preheat oven to 425°F.

Whisk together olive oil, lemon, lime, garlic and oregano in a small bowl and mix well. Add sliced cherry tomatoes, shallots and olives, mix well.

Place salmon fillets onto a parchment-lined baking dish. Spread the olive-tomato mixture onto the salmon, coating it entirely.

Bake for 20 minutes or until salmon flakes easily.

Serve each fillet topped with the tomato-olive mixture.

☑ Smart Facts

What are shallots?
Shallots are from the onion family and grow in clusters like garlic. Shallots are small and elongated onions, covered with a reddish or gray colored skin. The flavour of shallots is slightly sweeter than onions and a little garlicky. You can find shallots in your local grocery store or farmers' market year round but are fresh in spring. If shallots are unavailable use the same quantity of the white bulb taken from a green onion or use 1 small onion to equal 3 shallots.

RECIPE HIGHLIGHTS

* Dairy Free
* Simple and Quick
* Low Glycemic
* No Added Refined Sugars
* Diabetic Friendly

☑ Nutritional Analysis

Amount Per Serving

Calories	473.04
Total Fat	19.11 g
Saturated Fat	2.81 g
Cholesterol	93.5 mg
Sodium	200.28 mg
Potassium	161.5 mg
Total Carbohydrates	37.8 g
Fibre	1.21 g
Sugar	0.22 g
Protein	39.36 g

Old Fashioned Fall Stew

Imagine coming home from a long day to the smell of a stew waiting for you.

Take your slow cooker out of the cupboard and use it for a tender and tasty stew that is chockful of vegetables in a rich tomato sauce. *Serves 4-6*

Ingredients

- 1 pound of stewing beef (1-inch cubes) visible fat removed
- 2 tablespoons of brown rice flour
- 1 tablespoon of olive oil
- 3 medium carrots, sliced thinly
- 1 cup of onions, diced
- 2 parsnips, sliced thinly
- 4 potatoes, cut into quarters (keep the peelings on)
- 3 cloves of minced garlic
- 1 bay leaf
- 2 teaspoons of Italian seasoning
- ½ teaspoon of sea salt and pepper
- 1 (14-ounce) can of crushed tomatoes
- 1 (12-ounce/341-milliliter) can of V8 juice

Directions

Coat beef with flour, shaking off excess. Heat olive oil in a large skillet. Working in batches, sear beef in a skillet over medium high heat until well browned on all sides. Do not crowd the meat or it will not sear properly and meat will turn out stringy. Remove beef and set aside.

Mix vegetables, seasonings, garlic, bay leaf, sea salt, pepper and beef in a slow cooker. Stir in canned tomatoes and V8 juice. Cover and cook on low for 8-9 hours or on high for 4 hours.

Discard bay leaf before serving. Serve with fresh gluten-free buns or bread.

☑ Smart Facts

If you desire a thicker stew, add 1 tablespoon of tapioca starch to 2 tablespoons of water and slowly add the mixture until desired thickness is reached.

Did you know that potatoes are an even better source of immune-boosting vitamin C than oranges? Most of the vitamin C is found in the skin so leave it on for maximum nutritional value.

RECIPE HIGHLIGHTS

* Simple and Quick
* Dairy Free
* No Added Refined Sugars
* High in Protein and Iron
* Diabetic Friendly
* Low Glycemic

☑ Nutritional Analysis

Amount Per Serving	
Calories	485
Total Fat	21 g
Saturated Fat	8 g
Cholesterol	52.9 mg
Sodium	251 mg
Potassium	169.9 mg
Carbohydrates	56.1 g
Fibre	8.1 g
Sugar	10.4 g
Protein	20.1 g

Roasted Pecan Encrusted Fish Sticks

This is a gluten-free healthy version of an upscale fish stick. I have been able to convert even the most anti-fish palettes with this recipe. The roasted pecans make the fish crispy and so delicious. It is one that even your children will enjoy! *Serves 4*

Ingredients

- 16 ounces of fresh or frozen Tilapia, Cod, Haddock, Sole or other mild, white fish
- ½ cup of Italian seasoned gluten-free bread crumbs
- ¾ cup of finely chopped pecans
- 2½ tablespoons of melted butter or coconut oil
- Sea salt to taste

Directions

Preheat oven to 450°F.

Rinse fish and pat dry. Cut fish against grain in 1-inch thick slices.

Combine bread crumbs and pecans in a shallow bowl. Coat fish slices in melted butter/oil and then roll in breadcrumb/pecan mixture until each side of fish is coated.

Place fish on a parchment-lined baking pan. Bake fish for 8-10 minutes or until crust is brown and fish is flakey. Season to taste with sea salt.

☑ Smart Facts

If you are unable to find gluten-free Italian bread crumbs, make your own by adding 1 teaspoon of Italian seasoning and 2 tablespoons of grated Parmesan cheese to ½ cup of gluten-free bread crumbs.

RECIPE HIGHLIGHTS

* Simple and Quick
* No Added Refined Sugars
* Diabetic Friendly
* Low Glycemic

☑ Nutritional Analysis

Amount Per Serving (3 fish sticks)	
Calories	395.04
Total Fat	22.22 g
Saturated Fat	6.13 g
Cholesterol	106.96 mg
Sodium	350 mg
Potassium	573.47 mg
Total Carbohydrates	13.11 g
Fibre	2. 7g
Sugar	1.68 g
Protein	31.57 g

Slowly Simmered Beef Fajitas

This is a meal I absolutely love to come home to—it's easy to prepare first thing in the morning and the welcoming aroma of garlic, coriander and chili powder greets you like an old friend at the end of a long day. *Serves 6*

Ingredients

- 1½ pounds of beef flank steak
- 1 large onion, chopped
- 1 large green and red bell pepper, cut into large pieces
- 3 cloves of garlic, minced
- 2 tablespoons of chili powder
- 2 tablespoons of ground coriander
- 2 teaspoons of red pepper flakes
- 1 (14½-ounce) can stewed tomatoes
- pinch of cinnamon

Directions

Combine chili powder, coriander, red pepper flakes and cinnamon in slow cooker with the flank steak and stir until meat is coated with spices. Add in the onion, bell pepper, minced garlic and stir. Add in the can of tomatoes. Cover and cook on low heat for 8-10 hours or high heat for 4-5 hours.

Remove meat from the slow cooker and shred. Return to cooker and keep warm.

To serve, use a slotted spoon and place about 3 tablespoons of the mixture in the centre of a warm corn tortilla.

Roll and serve, use the remaining cooking juices as a dip.

☑ Smart Facts

RECIPE HIGHLIGHTS

* Simple and Quick
* Dairy Free
* High in Iron
* No Added Refined Sugars
* High in Protein

☑ Nutritional Analysis

Amount Per Serving	
Calories	284.22
Calories From Fat	94.49
Total Fat	10.52 g
Saturated Fat	3.77 g
Cholesterol	89.59 mg
Sodium	267.06 mg
Potassium	783.93 mg
Total Carbohydrates	12.46 g
Fibre	3.7 g
Sugar	5.56 g
Protein	34.96 g

Filet of Sole Almandine

Serves 4

Ingredients

- 4 - 4 ounce fillets of fresh sole
- 2 tablespoons olive oil
- ½ cup of toasted, slivered almonds
- Sea salt and pepper to taste
- Juice of ½ lemon

Directions

Preheat oven to 350 °F.

Rinse fish with cold water and pat dry. Brush fillets lightly with olive oil. Place fish in parchment lined baking dish, sprinkle with almonds. Squeeze lemon juice on the fillets.

Bake for 12 minutes or until fish is flakey when pricked with a fork. Season to taste with salt and pepper.

This is excellent with brown rice pilaf and sautéed vegetables.

☑ Smart Facts

The Journal of the American Medical Association reported a study by Brigham and Women's Hospital that eating at least 1 meal of fish weekly can cut the risk of sudden cardiac death in men in half! Fish is clearly a healthy addition to any diet.

☑ Nutritional Analysis

Amount Per Serving

Calories	265.5
Total Fat	14.22g
Saturated Fat	1.58g
Cholesterol	77.11mg
Sodium	119.31mg
Potassium	518.81mg
Total Carbohydrates	3.33g
Fiber	2.04g
Sugar	0.85g
Protein	31.21g

Brad's Burkey Burgers

I made these burgers as a compromise for my husband craving red meat and myself wanting to cut down on the saturated fat. These are simple and great burgers. They are a healthy compromise for those wanting the red meat taste but trying to cut down on their waistline.
Makes 8 burgers

Ingredients

- 1 pound of extra lean ground beef
- 1 pound of lean ground turkey
- 3 green onions, sliced thin
- 1 Tablespoon of Montreal Steak Spice
- ½ teaspoon of cayenne pepper (optional)
- ½ cup of gluten-free oatmeal
- 1 egg, slightly scrambled

Directions

Combine all of the above and make into small or large patties and grill on the BBQ.

☑ Smart Facts

RECIPE HIGHLIGHTS

* Easy to Make
* No Added Refined Sugars
* Dairy Free
* Low Glycemic
* High in Protein
* Wheat and Glu ten Free
* Diabetic Friendly
* Reduced Saturated Fat

☑ Nutritional Analysis

Amount Per Serving
Serving size: 1/8 of a recipe (4.5 ounces). Percent daily values based on the Reference Daily Intake (RDI) for a 2000 calorie diet. Nutrition information calculated from recipe ingredients.

Calories	237.74	
Calories From Fat (58%)	138.61	
% Daily Value		
Total Fat	15.16g	23%
Saturated Fat	5.36g	27%
Cholesterol	110.35mg	37%
Sodium	179.28mg	7%
Potassium	331.65mg	9%
Total Carbohydrates	2.3g	<1%
Fiber	0.39g	2%
Sugar	0.28g	
Protein	21.74g	43%

Gluten-Free Tourtière

Just like my mom and my grandmamma taught me...traditional French Canadian cusine....with ketchup no less! I can remember having this every Christmas season on both Christmas Eve and Christmas Day. I can still remember the labour and love that would go in every one... such wonderful memories.

Ingredients

- .5 lb each of lean ground beef, ground lamb and ground pork
- 1 onion, diced
- 2 garlic cloves, minced
- 1 ½ teaspoons sea salt
- ½ teaspoon each of dry thyme and sage
- ½ teaspoon of black pepper
- Pinch of ground cloves
- Gluten-Free Pie Crust Recipe

Directions

Cook all of the above in man on medium to high heat until cooked.

Drain off all the fat by tipping the pan to one side and then drain all the fat by putting the meat in a strainer and allow to sit for a minute or 2.

Put one crust down, fill up with meat filling and cover the second half with pie crust. Make sure to add little holes on the top crust in the middle to allow steam to vent.

Bake the pie for about 30 minutes. Let stand for 10 minutes before serving

☑ Smart Facts

Tourtière is not exclusive to Quebec. Tourtière is a traditional French-Canadian dish served by generations of French-Canadian families throughout Canada and the bordering areas of the United States. In the New England region of the U.S., especially in Maine, Rhode Island, Vermont, and New Hampshire, early 20th century immigrants from Quebec introduced the dish.

RECIPE HIGHLIGHTS

* Dairy Free
* Gluten-Free
* No Added Refined Sugars

☑ Nutritional Analysis

This falls under my grandmama's rule of "Tourtière's calories don't count- just go for a walk in the snow after..." I had to honour that. BUT make sure to go for a walk after to burn those extra potential calories.

Creamy Lemon
Dill Chicken

This is such an elegant meal. The creamy dill
infused sauce is rich and fragrant, and is a
beautiful complement to the lemon flavor.

Serve with a mixture of steamed brown and
wild rice, with sautéed peppers on the side!
I like to add a fresh sprig of dill on top of each
plate for a quick finishing touch. *Serves 4*

Ingredients

- 4 - 4 ounce chicken breasts, tilapia,
  cod or salmon fillets
- 2 garlic cloves, crushed
- 1 tablespoon of butter or olive oil
- ½ cup sour cream or Greek Yogurt,
  or dairy-free alternative
- 1-2 tablespoons of fresh dill, chopped with
  1 added tablespoon of fresh lemon juice

Directions

Preheat oven to 350 degrees.

Place fish in a casserole pan. Sprinkle lemon
juice, olive oil, garlic, salt and pepper over the
fish. Then cover with foil.

Bake in the oven for about 10-15 minutes until
the chicken or fish is moist and flakey.

Combine sour cream and dill in a bowl.

To serve, place each fillet on a plate, and top
with dill cream. Add salt and pepper to taste.

☑ Smart Facts

RECIPE HIGHLIGHTS
- * Simple and Quick
- * No Added Refined Sugars
- * Gluten and Wheat Free
- * Diabetic Friendly
- * Low Glycemic

☑ Nutritional Analysis

Amount Per Serving		
Calories		241.73
Calories From Fat (45%)		109.78
% Daily Value		
Total Fat	12.42g	19%
Saturated Fat	5.28g	26%
Cholesterol	77.29mg	26%
Sodium	79.35mg	3%
Potassium	494.6mg	14%
Total Carbohydrates	2.73g	<1%
Fiber	0.08g	<1%
Sugar	0.34g	
Protein	30.71g	61%

Cauliflower Crust Pizza

Moist, chewy and soft pizza crust made from... cauliflower? This is a dish you need to try to believe!! *Serves 6*

Ingredients

- 1 cup cooked, riced cauliflower
- 1 cup shredded mozzarella cheese
- 1 egg, beaten
- 1 teaspoon dried oregano
- ½ each of teaspoon minced garlic and sea salt
- olive oil (optional)
- pizza sauce, shredded cheese and your choice of toppings*

Directions

Remove stems and leaves from 1 head of cauliflower, and chop the florets into chunks.

Add floret chunks to your food processor, and pulse until it looks like grain. Do not overdo the pulse, or you will puree it. Alternatively, you can use a cheese grater.

Steam the riced cauliflower on low heat with a cover on (water is not needed). Cook for about 5 minutes.

To make the pizza crust:

Preheat oven to 450 degrees. Line a cookie sheet or a pizza pan with parchment paper.

In a medium bowl, stir together 1 cup of cauliflower, the beaten egg and mozzarella. Add oregano, minced garlic and salt, and mix well.

Transfer the mixture to your cookie sheet, and pat out into a 9" round pizza pan.

Bake at 450 degrees for 15 minutes.

Remove from oven and allow to cool. This helps to make the crust more solid.

☑ Smart Facts

A cup of boiled cauliflower delivers about 3.35 g of dietary fiber, which helps clean your digestive system and gets rid of unnecessary substances.

RECIPE HIGHLIGHTS

* Easy to Make
* No Added Refined Sugars
* Gluten and Wheat Free
* Full of antioxidants
* Diabetic Friendly

☑ Nutritional Analysis

Amount Per 1/6 serving of pizza	
Calories	73.08
Calories From Fat (53%)	
Total Fat	4.37g
Saturated Fat	2.49g
Cholesterol	49.33mg
Sodium	309.59mg
Potassium	85.25mg
Total Carbohydrates	1.8g
Fiber	0.53g
Sugar	0.73g
Protein	6.76g

To make the pizza:

Add the sauce, toppings and cheese. Place the pizza under a broiler at a high heat just until the cheese is melted (approximately 3 to 4 minutes).

*Toppings need to be precooked since you are only broiling for a few minutes.

Maple Grilled Salmon

Ingredients

- 4 – 4 ounce pieces of salmon
- 4 Tablespoons maple syrup
- 2 Tablespoons Bragg's All Purpose Seasoning*
- 4 teaspoons sesame seeds
- 4 Tablespoons sesame oil

  Braggs can be found at your health food store

Directions

Combine all liquid ingredients and sesame seeds and place salmon in a Ziploc Bag and marinate for 24 hours. Grill salmon until done and serve with toasted sesame seeds on top with a drizzle of sesame oil.

☑ Smart Facts

RECIPE HIGHLIGHTS
* Gluten and Wheat-Free
* Diabetic Friendly
* Dairy Free

☑ Nutritional Analysis

Amount Per Serving	
Calories	227
Calories From Fat	165
Total Fat:	18.6g
Cholesterol	17.9mg
Sodium	318.5mg
Potassium	159.5mg
Carbohydrates	8.2g
Fiber	<1g
Sugar	6.1g
Protein	7.3g

Spicy Curry Chicken with Creamy Peanut Sauce

Ingredients

Curry Chicken

- 2 boneless skinless chicken breasts cubed
- 2 teaspoons curry powder
- 4 Tablespoons each of wheat free tamari, lemon juice and honey
- 2 cloves of garlic-crushed
- ½ teaspoon cayenne pepper
- 1 large onion sliced

Creamy Peanut Sauce

- 4 Tablespoons each of honey, wheat free tamari and coconut milk
- Mix the above thoroughly over low heat

Directions

Cube 2 chicken breasts into bit size pieces. Combine all of curry chicken ingredients in a Ziploc bag and leave overnight or minimum 30 minutes (the longer the more the spices with integrate into the chicken).

Bake chicken in marinade in a covered dish at 350 for 1 hour.

Serve chicken with marinade over brown rice and drizzle with the above peanut sauce.

Turkey Burgers

These burgers are great with sweet potato wedge fries! Perfect with a gluten-free bun, mustard, lettuce and fresh tomato. *Serves 4*

Ingredients

- 1 pound of ground turkey
- ½ cup of feta cheese, crumbled
- 2 tablespoons of fresh chopped basil, (or 2 teaspoons dried)
- 1 large clove of garlic, minced
- ⅓ cup of crushed almonds, toasted
- ¼ cup of gluten-free bread crumbs
- Sea salt and pepper to taste
- Olive oil for grill

Directions

Preheat BBQ to medium-high heat.

In a mixing bowl, mix ground turkey, cheese, basil, garlic, nuts, bread crumbs, sea salt and pepper until well combined. Divide mixture into four 1-inch thick patties.

Lightly oil the grill. Grill the patties with the BBQ cover closed for about 6 minutes per side or until no longer pink.

Serve on gluten-free buns.

☑ Smart Facts

RECIPE HIGHLIGHTS

* Simple and Quick
* Egg Free
* High in Protein
* Low Glycemic
* Diabetic Friendly
* No Added Refined Sugars

☑ Nutritional Analysis

Amount Per Serving

Calories	268.59
Total Fat	13.11 g
Saturated	2.65 g
Cholesterol	57.84 mg
Sodium	347.19 mg
Potassium	466.28 mg
Total Carbohydrates	7.62 g
Fibre	1.31 g
Sugar	2.5 g
Protein	23.91 g

Side Dishes

Side dishes add a whole different flavour dimension to any dish. Each of these sides will easily compliment any one of the mains in this book. As always I've focussed on vegetables or whole grains for these recipes.

List of recipes:

- Baked Sweet Potato Fries
- Healthy Guacamole
- Perfectly Smooth Mashed Potatoes
- Quinoa Tabouleh
- Ratatouille
- Roasted Acorn Squash
- Roasted Baby Bok Choy
- Roasted Butternut Squash and Quinoa Risotto
- Roasted Root Vegetables
- Sautéed Rainbow Peppers with Swiss Chard

- Spicy Spaghetti squash
- Fresh and Spicy Mango and Strawberry Salsa
- Gluten-Free stuffing
- Maca Energy Balls
- Cranberry Fat Flush
- Green Machine Vegetable Juice
- Healthy Vitamin Waters
- Krazy for Kale
- Pumpkin Spice Butter
- Warming Black Bean Dip

Baked Sweet Potato Fries

I cannot even begin to tell you about the love affair I have with sweet potatoes. To me, sweet potatoes are the ultimate of comfort foods. These fries are sweet, crispy and so comforting!
Serves 4

Ingredients

- 2 large sweet potatoes
- 2 tablespoons of olive oil
- Sea salt and pepper

Directions

Preheat oven to 425°F.

Cut sweet potatoes into large batonnets like French fries. Place in a large bowl or Ziploc bag, add the olive oil, sea salt and pepper. Mix to completely coat the sweet potato fries.

Place on baking sheet in a single layer.

Bake in preheated oven for 15 minutes. Turn fries and bake for another 10 minutes until tender and crispy.

☑ Smart Facts

Sweet potatoes are an excellent source of beta carotene making it the perfect comfort food to help build up your immune system.

RECIPE HIGHLIGHTS

* Simple and Quick
* No Added Refined Sugars
* Diabetic Friendly
* Low Glycemic
* Vegetarian and Vegan

☑ Nutritional Analysis

Amount Per Serving

Calories	115.57
Total Fat	6.78 g
Saturated Fat	0.94 g
Cholesterol	0 mg
Sodium	35.89 mg
Potassium	219.12 mg
Total Carbohydrates	13.08 g
Fibre	1.95 g
Sugar	2.72 g
Protein	1.02 g

Healthy Guacamole

I first made this guacamole for my husband's 40th birthday party with baked corn chips. Everyone kept asking "Who brought the guac—it's awesome!" Who doesn't love a good guacamole?! *Serves 6*

Ingredients

- 2 ripe avocados peeled and seeded
- 2 green onions, chopped
- 4 tablespoons of fresh lime juice
- 1 clove of garlic, crushed
- ½ jalapeno pepper, finely chopped
- ½ teaspoon of sea salt and pepper
- ½ teaspoon of cumin
- 1 medium tomato, diced
- Fresh cilantro chopped to garnish

Directions

In a food processor, purée avocados, onions, garlic, jalapeno pepper, and lime juice using the pulse setting. When well combined, adjust seasoning with sea salt, pepper and cumin. Keep mixture refrigerated until ready to serve. Just before serving stir in chopped tomatoes and garnish with cilantro.

Serve with organic corn chips. It can also be used as a dip with raw vegetables or a spread on your favourite sandwich.

☑ Smart Facts

Interestingly, the avocado is actually a fruit although we use it mostly as a vegetable. The fat found in the avocado is the heart healthy monounsaturated fat. This heart healthy fat actually helps to lower the "bad" cholesterol, LDL without lowering the "good " cholesterol, HDL.

The avocado also contains vitamins A, D, and E, 14 minerals and contains more potassium than bananas.

RECIPE HIGHLIGHTS
* Simple and Quick
* Egg Free
* Dairy Free
* No Added Refined Sugars
* Vegan and Vegetarian

☑ Nutritional Analysis

Amount Per Serving

Calories	106.13
Calories From Fat	75.18
Total Fat	8.96 g
Saturated Fat	1.24 g
Cholesterol	0 mg
Sodium	163.62 mg
Potassium	378.83 mg
Total Carbohydrates	7.46 g
Fibre	4.46 g
Sugar	1.11 g
Protein	1.53 g

Perfectly Smooth Mashed Potatoes

Mashed potatoes are the ultimate comfort food. This recipe is oh so fluffy, creamy and satisfying. Mashed potatoes make me happy! My mother came up with this recipe for me when she found out that I was allergic to milk when I was a little girl. It is still one of my all time favourites! *Serves 8*

Ingredients

- 6 medium size Yukon Gold potatoes, with skins on
- 1 teaspoon of sea salt
- ½ cup of reserved potato water
- 2 tablespoons of butter or olive oil
- 1 egg, slightly beaten
- Sea salt and black pepper to taste
- Pinch of ground nutmeg (Mom's family secret)

Optional Add In:
- ½ cup of sliced green onions or chopped chives

Directions

Put potatoes and sea salt in a large pot and fill with cold water until water just covers the potatoes. Cook the potatoes uncovered on medium-high heat until water comes to a boil. Once boiling, reduce heat to medium-low and simmer for 20 minutes or until potatoes are tender.

Turn off heat and strain potatoes, reserving ½ cup of the potato water for later use. Return potatoes to the pot, cover and let rest for 5 minutes on the cooling burner. This will help the potatoes to become fluffy.

Add 2 tablespoons butter or olive oil, egg, sea salt, pepper and nutmeg (the egg will cook in the heat of the potatoes and give them a creamy texture). Quickly begin mashing potatoes adding reserved potato water a little at a time while mashing until desired texture and consistency are reached.

☑ Smart Facts

I keep the potato skins on when I make mashed potatoes for 3 really good reasons:

1. They taste really good.

2. Most of the nutrition is in the potato skin.

3. It is less labour intensive!

RECIPE HIGHLIGHTS

* Simple and Quick
* Dairy Free
* No Added Refined Sugars
* Vegetarian

☑ Nutritional Analysis

Amount Per Serving

Calories	140.83
Total Fat	3.64 g
Saturated Fat	2.06 g
Cholesterol	34.07 mg
Sodium	272.93 mg
Potassium	590.48 mg
Total Carbohydrates	24.18 g
Fibre	3.04 g
Sugar	1.14 g
Protein	3.61 g

Quinoa Tabouleh

A refreshing side dish that compliments fish, chicken, lamb or beef with both its colour and minty flavour. *Serves 8*

Ingredients

- 1 cup of quinoa
- 1¾ cups of water
- ½ teaspoon of sea salt
- ¼ cup of olive oil
- ¼ cup of lemon juice
- Sea salt and pepper to taste
- ½ red pepper, diced
- ½ yellow pepper, diced
- ½ cup of fresh, chopped mint or 3 tablespoons dried
- 2 cups of parsley, finely chopped
- 1 cup of green onions, finely diced
- 1 small carrot, grated

Directions

Wash and drain quinoa. Place quinoa, water and sea salt in a pot and bring to a boil on medium-high heat. Cover pot and simmer for 20-25 minutes and allow to cool.

In a large bowl, whisk olive oil and lemon juice adding sea salt and pepper to taste. Add all of the vegetables and toss well until all ingredients are thoroughly combined. Add cooled quinoa and toss again until well combined.

Serve at room temperature.

☑ Smart Facts

RECIPE HIGHLIGHTS

* High in Protein
* Diabetic Friendly
* Egg Free
* Low Glycemic
* Diabetic Friendly
* No Added Refined Sugars
* Vegetarian and Vegan

☑ Nutritional Analysis

Amount Per Serving

Calories	179.51
Total Fat	4 g
Saturated Fat	1.43 g
Cholesterol	0 mg
Sodium	373.79 mg
Potassium	327.12 mg
Total Carbohydrates	18.49 g
Fibre	3.02 g
Sugar	1.46 g
Protein	4.04 g

Ratatouille

I rediscovered ratatouille after the Pixar movie *Ratatouille* was released. That movie inspired me to want to show people "that anyone can cook!" Anyone can cook and it can be fun and easy! Enjoy this inspirational dish. *Serves 6*

Ingredients

- 2 tablespoons of olive oil
- 1 onion, chopped
- 4 cloves of garlic, minced
- 1 large eggplant, cubed
- 1 (14-ounce) can stewed tomatoes
- 2 small zucchini, cut into large chunks
- 1 teaspoon of dried oregano
- Sea salt and pepper to taste

Directions

Heat olive oil on medium heat in a medium saucepan. Add onions and garlic and sauté until soft. Add eggplant and tomatoes and simmer uncovered until softened. Add zucchini and oregano and continue to simmer for an additional 10-15 minutes.

Season with sea salt and pepper to taste.

☑ Smart Facts

To ensure the best results possible for the ratatouille, use the freshest vegetables you can find either from your own garden or farmers' market.

Eggplant — Make sure to select medium sized eggplants with dark, glossy skin. The eggplant should be firm and heavy.

Zucchini — You want them small, young and not shriveled. Make sure you can still see the end of a fresh green stem. If you have a garden then pick them the same day you plan to prepare the dish.

RECIPE HIGHLIGHTS

* Simple and Quick
* Dairy Free
* No Added Refined Sugars
* High in Fibre
* Vegetarian and Vegan

☑ Nutritional Analysis

Amount Per Serving

Calories	80.03
Total Fat	2.7 g
Saturated Fat	0.39 g
Cholesterol	0 mg
Sodium	177.24 mg
Potassium	514.54 mg
Total Carbohydrates	14.02 g
Fibre	4.8 g
Sugar	6.43 g
Protein	2.48 g

Roasted Acorn Squash

My mother used to make her own baby food and one of my first foods was roasted acorn squash. I still have the same craving for it that I developed at infancy—only now I can eat an entire squash on my own.

I created this recipe just as an experiment in one of my cooking classes and the students all raved that this was their favorite one during the course!

Enjoy—for infants and adults alike! *Serves 4*

Ingredients

- 1 acorn squash cut in half, seeds removed
- 2 Mejool dates
- 1 tablespoon of butter or coconut oil
- ½ teaspoon of Garam Masala

Directions

Preheat oven to 375°F.

Place acorn squash flesh side up on baking sheet. Add 1 date in the cavity of each halved squash. Add butter/coconut oil to the side of each date. Sprinkle Garam Masala on both sides of squash.

Bake in the oven for 35-45 minutes or until yellow flesh is soft and edges are a golden brown.

☑ Smart Facts

Did you know squash is officially a fruit and the smaller the squash the more flavoursome it will be. Squash is an excellent source of fibre and vitamin A. A 1 cup serving of acorn squash delivers 145% of your daily recommended intake of vitamin A.

RECIPE HIGHLIGHTS

* Simple and Quick
* No Added Refined Sugars
* Low Glycemic
* Diabetic Friendly
* Vegetarian and Vegan

☑ Nutritional Analysis

Amount Per Serving	
Calories	101.79
Total Fat	3.01 g
Saturated Fat	1.85 g
Cholesterol	7.63 mg
Sodium	23.8 mg
Potassium	458.26 mg
Total Carbohydrates	20.23 g
Fibre	2.42 g
Sugar	7.98 g
Protein	1.11 g

Roasted Baby Bok Choy

I just love the simplicity of this side dish. We often do not get enough greens in our diet and this is a simple way to boost up both our fibre and our greens. *Serves 4.*

Ingredients

- 1 pound of baby bok choy
- 2 tablespoons of olive oil
- ½ of teaspoon of each sea salt and pepper
- Lemon juice to taste

Directions

Preheat oven to 400°F.

Wash bok choy thoroughly and pat dry with paper towel so no water remains.

Toss bok choy in olive oil and sea salt and pepper in a large bowl until thoroughly coated.

Place bok choy on a baking sheet in a thin layer - do not allow bok choy to overlap.

Roast in oven for 8-10 minutes.

For additional flavour you can squeeze ½ a lemon atop the bok choy.

☑ Smart Facts

Bok Choy is an excellent source of calcium. One cup of bok choy contains as much calcium as ½ cup of milk!

Bok Choy is also part of the Brassica family of vegetables (like cabbage). This family of vegetables contains phytochemicals called 'indoles' which are believed to deactivate potent estrogens that can stimulate the growth of tumours—especially in the breast.

RECIPE HIGHLIGHTS

* Simple and Quick
* Dairy Free
* No Added Refined Sugars
* Vegetarian and Vegan
* Diabetic Friendly

☑ Nutritional Analysis

Amount Per Serving

Calories	49.78
Total Fat	3.72 g
Saturated Fat	0.51 g
Cholesterol	0 mg
Sodium	244.26 mg
Potassium	283.44 mg
Total Carbohydrates	3.9 g
Fibre	2.45 g
Sugar	1.35 g
Protein	1.42 g

Roasted Butternut Squash and Quinoa Risotto

Enjoy the creaminess of the Arborio rice combined with curry, buttery squash and quinoa. *Serves 8*

Ingredients

- 1 small butternut squash, halved and seeds removed
- 1 teaspoon of olive oil or butter
- 1 teaspoon of honey
- 4 cups of chicken or vegetable broth
- 1 tablespoon of melted butter or coconut oil
- 1 cup of onions, chopped fine
- 3 cloves of garlic, minced
- 2 sprigs of fresh thyme
- Zest ½ a lemon
- 1 cup of Arborio rice
- ½ cup of quinoa
- ½ teaspoon of curry powder
- 1 tablespoon of butter, coconut or olive oil
- Sea salt and pepper to taste

Directions

Preheat oven to 400°F.

Whisk together melted butter/olive oil and honey in a small bowl and brush the cut side of the squash, coat it completely. Place cut side down on parchment-lined baking sheet. Roast squash until tender (20-35 minutes), remove from oven. Scoop out flesh and purée.

Meanwhile, add 4 cups of chicken broth to a medium sauce pan and bring to a boil and then reduce heat to simmer. Melt 1 tablespoon of butter/oil of choice in a large saucepan. Add onions and garlic and cook gently on medium heat for 3-4 minutes without browning, stir occasionally. Add the rice and quinoa. Continue cooking for 3 minutes, stir continually. Add in

Do not let the directions or the title scare you. The trick to a perfect risotto is the constant stirring. If you can constantly stir, you can create the perfect risotto!

RECIPE HIGHLIGHTS

* Dairy Free, if using coconut oil
* Diabetic Friendly
* Low Glycemic
* Vegetarian

☑ Nutritional Analysis

Amount Per Serving	
Calories	199.91
Total Fat	5.13 g
Saturated Fat	1.53 g
Cholesterol	3.82 mg
Sodium	53.17 mg
Potassium	292.84 mg
Total Carbohydrates	32.95 g
Fibre	1.72 g
Sugar	2.33 g
Protein	6.18 g

thyme. Start adding hot chicken broth in ½ cup increments, stir constantly. Maintain heat on both the stock and the rice mixture so that both are simmering. Continue adding stock, stir continuously and cook mixture until quinoa is soft and rice becomes al dante (20 minutes). Reduce heat to low.

Add 3-4 cups of squash to the risotto and stir thoroughly. Add curry powder, lemon zest, and butter.

Roasted Root Vegetables

I love the simplicity of this recipe, and yet every time I make it, I always get recipe requests. It is one of those recipes that is a failsafe side dish and will make any regular meal taste comforting and filling. *Serves 6*

Ingredients

- 6 cups of mixed root vegetables, peeled and cut into chunks (2 cups of sweet potatoes, 1 cup of baby carrots, 1 cup of parsnips and 2 cups of potatoes)
- 2 tablespoons of olive oil
- 2 teaspoons of Montreal Steak Spice

Directions

Preheat oven to 400°F.

Mix together vegetables, olive oil and spice in a large bowl until well combined.

Place vegetable mixture onto a large parchment-lined cookie sheet in one layer. Cookie sheet should have a rim. Roast in the oven for 45-60 minutes, stirring once or twice until vegetables are golden in colour and tender. Do not be alarmed if the bottom of the vegetables becomes a little brown. These are the natural sugars of the vegetables caramelizing.

☑ Smart Facts

RECIPE HIGHLIGHTS

* Simple and Quick
* Dairy Free
* No Added Refined Sugars
* Low Glycemic
* Diabetic Friendly
* Vegetarian and Vegan

☑ Nutritional Analysis

Amount Per Serving

Calories	156.88
Total Fat	4.64 g
Saturated Fat	0.65 g
Cholesterol	0 mg
Sodium	99.85 mg
Potassium	665.91 mg
Total Carbohydrates	27.58 g
Fibre	3.82 g
Sugar	3.79 g
Protein	2.47 g

Sautéed Rainbow Peppers and Swiss Chard

This simple side dish compliments any fish or chicken recipe very well. The bright contrast of colours from the red, yellow and green catch the eye. Many times one can find 'Rainbow' Swiss Chard at your local farmers' market in the summer time making this dish all the more colourful! *Serves 4*

Ingredients

- 2 tablespoons of olive oil
- 1 Spanish onion, sliced into rings
- 2 cloves of garlic, minced
- 1 red, orange, yellow and green pepper cut into slices
- 1 large bunch of Swiss Chard (middle stems removed) chopped finely (approximately 4 cups)
- Sea salt and pepper to taste.

Directions

Heat olive oil in a large pan on medium-high heat.

Add onions and allow to cook until they start to become soft. Add garlic and sauté with onions for 1-2 minutes. Add peppers and allow peppers to sauté with onions for 10 minutes or until they become soft. Right before serving add the Swiss Chard and stir into the pepper, onion mixture until they begin to wilt. Add sea salt and pepper to taste.

Serve immediately.

☑ Smart Facts

Swiss Chard is second only to spinach as being the World's Healthiest Vegetable. Swiss Chard is high in calcium, magnesium and vitamin K making it an excellent bone builder. Multiple studies are also showing Swiss Chard's unique ability for blood sugar stabilization due to its high fibre content and ability to slow down the breakdown of carbohydrates into sugar.

RECIPE HIGHLIGHTS

* Simple and Quick
* Dairy Free
* No Added Refined Sugars
* Diabetic Friendly
* Low Glycemic

☑ Nutritional Analysis

Amount Per Serving	
Calories	118.73
Total Fat	7.23 g
Saturated Fat	1 g
Cholesterol	0 mg
Sodium	82.61 mg
Potassium	436.04 mg
Total Carbohydrates	12.56 g
Fibre	3.56 g
Sugar	4.33 g
Protein	2.45 g

Earthy Nut Loaf

Meat loaf was a meal that our family would always look forward to...My dad would slather ketchup on it and always fight for those crispy burnt pieces. This is a vegan version of that same recipe but using only whole plant based foods. *Serves 12*

Ingredients

- 2 large onions, finely chopped
- 2 garlic cloves, minced
- 1 ¼ cup chopped mushrooms
- ¼ cup finely chopped green pepper
- 2 Tablespoons olive oil
- 3 cups organic carrots, grated
- 1 ½ cup organic celery, chopped
- ¾ cup flax meal (mixed with 1¼ cup water and let sit)
- ½ cup + 1 Tablespoon chopped organic walnuts
- ¼ cup sunflower seeds
- ½ teaspoon sea salt
- 2 teaspoons each of dried oregano and basil
- 1 teaspoon pepper
- 3 cups soft gluten-free bread crumbs

☑ Smart Facts

Phytonutrient research on the antioxidant and anti-inflammatory benefits of walnuts has moved this food further and further up the ladder of foods that are protective against metabolic syndrome, cardiovascular problems, and type 2 diabetes.

☑ Nutritional Analysis

Amount Per Serving

Calories	182.17
Total Fat	11.8g
Saturated Fat	1.26g
Cholesterol	0mg
Sodium	193.77mg
Potassium	350.12mg
Total Carbohydrates	16.43g
Fiber	5.37g
Sugar	3.91g
Protein	4.97g

Directions

In an iron skillet, heat well on medium heat, and sprinkle a slight amount of salt in the skillet. Then add 2 teaspoons of olive oil to coat the pan. This will help to make a 'non-stick' coating.

Add onions and garlic to heated skillet, and sauté until soft.

Add olive oil, mushrooms and green peppers, and cook until tender.

In a bowl, combine the mushroom mixture, carrots, celery, flax meal mixture, walnuts, sunflower seeds, sea salt, basil, oregano and pepper. Mix well.

Add gluten-free breadcrumbs, and combine well.

Coat a 9" x 5" x 3" pan with olive oil. Then line the pan with parchment paper. This will ensure it won't stick. Transfer the veggie mixture to the prepared pan. Bake at 350 degrees for 1 hour. In the last 20 minutes of baking add your favorite gluten-free BBQ sauce to the top of the loaf. Allow loaf to sit for 10 minutes before slicing.

Fresh and Spicy Mango and Strawberry Salsa

This salsa is excellent served with corn tortilla chips or as a side salsa with chicken or beef. You can even veg it up by adding a can of black beans to it for a complete meal. Spicy, Fresh and Sweet- all in the same bite!

Serves 8 with ½ cup for each person

Ingredients

- 2 cups diced mango (if you do not have mangos you can use fresh pineapple as well)
- 2 cups of sliced strawberries
- 1 teaspoon of red pepper flakes (or more if you like heat)
- 4 Tablespoons of chopped fresh cilantro+ chopped red onion
- 2 tablespoons fresh lime juice
- Sea salt to taste

Directions

Gently stir all ingredients together and season with salt.

☑ Smart Facts

Cilantro is one of the richest herbal sources for vitamin K; provides about 258% of DRI. Vitamin-K has potential role in bone mass building by promoting osteotrophic activity in the bones. It also has established role in the treatment of Alzheimer's disease patients by limiting neuronal damage in their brain.

RECIPE HIGHLIGHTS

* Easy to Make
* Dairy Free
* Gluten-Free
* High in Vitamin C
* Low in Saturated Fat
* No Added Refined Sugars
* Vegetarian

☑ Nutritional Analysis

Amount Per ½ cup Serving		
Calories	41.99	
Calories From Fat (5%)	2.01	
% Daily Value		
Total Fat	0.24g	<1%
Saturated Fat	0.03g	<1%
Cholesterol	0mg	0%
Sodium	60.94mg	3%
Potassium	134.32mg	4%
Total Carbohydrates	10.7g	4%
Fiber	1.64g	7%
Sugar	8.03g	
Protein	0.56g	1%

Simply Smart Gluten-Free Stuffing

This is a simple stuffing recipe that I have been making since I could safely use a knife. My mother would prop me up to the kitchen counter, have me stand on the chair and make this recipe. My older brother would often come in and steal the bacon just to hear me holler at him! This recipe just lets the flavors speak for themselves with what my mother calls the 'Holy Trinity' of French Canadian Cooking- celery, carrots and onions.

Ingredients

- 4 slices of gluten-free turkey bacon
- 6 cups of diced gluten-free bread cubes either toasted in the oven or left out overnight
- 3 large ribs celery, medium diced
- 1 cup each of cooking onions and carrots, chopped fine
- 2 Tablespoons of olive oil, butter or coconut oil
- 1 teaspoon of dried sage+½ teaspoon of dried thyme+ salt and pepper to taste½ cup of gluten-free vegetable or chicken stock

Directions

Add turkey bacon to a medium heated pan and cook until crispy. Set bacon aside and allow to cool. Chop into small pieces when cooled.

Sautee the holy trinity of celery, onions and carrots in oil/butter on medium to low heat until the vegetables soften. Add the crumbled bacon, bread spices, chicken stock and salt and pepper and mix thoroughly for 1-2 minutes in the pan. Remove from heat. Place all of the ingredients either in a greased casserole dish or stuff in turkey. If in a dish, bake covered with foil for 15 minutes at 425 degrees F and then remove foil and bake for an additional 10 minutes

☑ Smart Facts

Sage is an herb that has been prized for thousands of years not just for its culinary uses but also for its nutritional properties. Sage is a good source of bone building calcium, blood building iron and blood pressure regulation potassium!

RECIPE HIGHLIGHTS

* Dairy Free
* Egg Free
* No Added Refined Sugars
* Gluten-Free
* Diabetic Friendly

☑ Nutritional Analysis

Amount Per Serving

Calories	107.93
Total Fat	4.04g
Saturated Fat	.51g
Cholesterol	4.31mg
Sodium	267.16mg
Potassium	139.96mg
Total Carbohydrates	14.24g
Fiber	1.5g
Sugar	2.38g
Protein	3.91g

High Energy Maca Balls

The combination of cinnamon, coconut and pumpkin seeds not only tastes amazing but is a perfect mid afternoon pick up or after workout re-energizer! *Makes 24 1-inch balls*

Ingredients

- 2 ½ cups gluten-free rolled oats regular or quick cooking
- ½ cup each of raw pumpkin seeds and golden raisins
- 2 teaspoons each of cinnamon and vanilla extract
- 3 Tablespoons each of ground Maca and unsweetened cocoa powder
- ½ cup each of almond butter and pure honey or maple syrup
- ¼ cup of ground flax seeds and shredded unsweetened coconut

Directions

Combine all dry ingredients except ground flax seeds and coconut. Put flaxseeds and coconut and spread on a plate. Mix all the wet ingredients thoroughly until well combined.

Moisten hands, and roll dough into 1-inch balls. Roll balls into ground flaxseeds or coconut and place in freezer 20 minutes to set, then serve or store in the fridge.

☑ Smart Facts

Maca is a traditional staple superfood-food-herb from the harsh cold climates of the high Andes in Peru that has been used for thousands of years.

Maca invigorates; rejuvenates the endocrine system; benefits the thyroid, the sexual organs, and the adrenals; supports brain health and good neurochemistry; helps fight feelings of depression– in short, it is one of the most incredible foods on the planet.

You can find maca at your local health food store

RECIPE HIGHLIGHTS

* Easy to Make
* High in Fibre
* Low in saturated fat
* Low Glycemic
* No Added Refined Sugars
* Vegetarian

☑ Nutritional Analysis

Amount Per Serving

Calories	97
Total Fat	3.6g
Cholesterol	0mg
Sodium	32.3mg
Potassium	111.7mg
Carbohydrates	16.1g
Fiber	1.2g
Sugar	8.2g
Protein	2.3g

Fat Flushing Cranberry Juice

This is an excellent tart juice to drink either hot or cold to stimulate the metabolism.
Serves 6

Ingredients

- 3 cups pure, unsweetened cranberry juice
- 3 cups water
- 3 inches worth sliced ginger
- ¼ cup fresh lemon juice
- 2 cinnamon sticks (about 3 inches each)
- maple syrup to taste

Directions

Combine all of the ingredients into a saucepan, and bring to a boil.

Simmer for 5 minutes.

Can be served warm or cold.

☑ Smart Facts

According to Certified Nutritional Scientist Ann Louise Gittleman, Ph.D., the organic acids of cranberry juice have an emulsifying effect on stored fat in the body.

Cranberries stimulate the metabolism to start using stored fat! Cranberry juice is also a natural diuretic, and can help rid one of extra water due to hormonal fluctuations and excess salt consumption.

This is also an excellent cocktail to help prevent bladder infections kidney stones.

RECIPE HIGHLIGHTS
* Simple and Quick
* Dairy Free
* No Added Refined Sugars
* High in Vitamin C
* Gluten and Wheat Free
* Vegetarian / Vegan

☑ Nutritional Analysis

Amount Per Serving

Calories	90.77
Total Fat	0g
Saturated Fat	0.g
Cholesterol	0mg
Sodium	5mg
Potassium	
Total Carbohydrates	24.17g
Fiber	1g
Sugar	14g
Protein	0g

Green Machine Vegetable Juice

I call this green machine juice as this vegetable juice gives me so much energy I feel like I can work out like a machine! Vegetable juicing is an incredible way to get in all the detoxifying properties of vegetables. 1 serving of this juice is the equivalent of eating over 5 cups of vegetables per glass!! Now enjoy the energy surge! *Serves 2*

Ingredients

- 6 leaves of Romaine lettuces
- 1 green apple or 1 cup of seedless green grapes
- 2 large carrots
- 1 English cucumber
- 4 celery stalks
- 2 small baby Bok Choy or 2 cups of baby spinach
- 1 cup of kale or asparagus
- 2 inch portion of fresh ginger root

Directions

Juice all of the above in a vegetable juicer.

Serve over ice and drink within 20 minutes.

☑ Smart Facts

This juice is an INCREDIBLE source of potassium- containing the equivilant potassium of over 3 small bananas.Potassium, is the synonym for health insurer. It contains the qualities for maintaining a high level of human well-being and a cheerful lifestyle. Apart from acting as an electrolyte, this mineral is required for keeping heart, brain, kidney, muscle tissues and other important organs of human body in good condition. Potassium also naturally lowers blood pressure.

RECIPE HIGHLIGHTS

* Dairy Free
* No Added Refined Sugars
* Vegetarian
* Vegan
* Full of Antioxidants
* Diabetic Friendly
* Potassium Rich

☑ Nutritional Analysis

Amount Per Serving	
Calories	136.68
Total Fat	1.43g
Saturated Fat	0.21g
Cholesterol	0mg
Sodium	120.2mg
Potassium	1305.34mg
Total Carbohydrates	30.38g
Fiber	11.87g
Sugar	15.94g
Protein	5.5g

Healthy Vitamin Waters!

I often hear clients that really struggle with drinking just plain water as they find it too bland. A typical ' vitamin water' has as much sugar as a chocolate bar! Eeek!!

So...i decided to Smarten things up a bit!

Here are some FUN water combinations.... calorie free, full of flavour and NO chemicals!

Fill a mason jar with pure filtered water and add one of the following combinations:

Metabolism Booster

- 1 cup of chopped fresh pineapple+ a large bunch a fresh mint- pineapple stimulates the digestion and aids in weight loss

Water Retention Blaster

- 1 cup of fresh watermelon+ large bunch of rosemary- watermelon is a natural diuretic

Hot Flash Rescue

- 1 cup of a mix of raspberries, cherries, blueberries of blackberries+ large bunch of Sage- Sage helps to regulate temperature and helps to reduce hot flushes in menopausal women- add 2 Tablespoons of ground flax if you like to boost support your hormones even more!

☑ Smart Facts

Water makes up more than two thirds of human body weight, and without water, we would die in a few days. The human brain is made up of 95% water, blood is 82% and lungs 90%. A mere 2% drop in our body's water supply can trigger signs of dehydration: fuzzy short-term memory, trouble with basic math, and difficulty focusing on smaller print, such as a computer screen. (Are you having trouble reading this? Drink up!)

Mild dehydration is also one of the most common causes of daytime fatigue. An estimated seventy-five percent of Americans have mild, chronic dehydration. Pretty scary statistic for a developed country where water is readily available through the tap or bottle water.

Krazzzy for Kale

You will not even believe how absolutely addictive these are! I serve them at cooking classes are are the first recipe to go.
Serves 6

Ingredients

- **1 bunch kale, washed and dried (crucial step!)**
- **1 Tablespoon olive oil**

  Flavor Variations:

- **Soy & Sesame: 2 Tablespoons Wheat Free Tamari sauce + 1 ½ Tablespoons sesame seeds**
- **Salt Lime & Chili: Juice of 1 lime + 1 teaspoon lime zest + 2 teaspoons chili powder**
- **Basic: 1 extra Tablespoon of olive oil + 1 teaspoon of sea salt**
- **Roasted Garlic: 3 cloves garlic, finely chopped + 3 teaspoons garlic salt**

Directions

Step 1: Preheat the oven to 300 degrees. Pour base ingredients into large Ziplock bag.

Step 2: Pour flavor ingredients in, and shake/smoosh until relatively combined.

Step 3: Remove kale stems, and chop into large-bite-sized pieces (they'll shrink a bit while baking). Put the kale in the bag – don't press the air out. And SHAKE IT⊠ Press all the air out and smoosh together.

Step 4; Lay kale on a lined baking sheet (or one that's sprayed lightly with cooking spray). Place in the oven for 30 minutes or until crisp.

☑ Smart Facts

Kale is high in Vitamin K. Eating a diet high in Vitamin K can help protect against various cancers. It is also necessary for a wide variety of bodily functions including normal bone health and the prevention of blood clotting. Also increased levels of vitamin K can help people suffering from Alzheimer's disease.

Kale is filled with powerful antioxidants. Antioxidants, such as carotenoids and flavonoids help protect against various cancers.

RECIPE HIGHLIGHTS
* Health Accolades
* Dairy Free
* Diabetic Friendly
* Egg Free
* No Added Refined Sugars
* Vegetarian
* Vegan

☑ Nutritional Analysis

Amount Per Serving		
Calories	28.22	
Calories From Fat (60%)	16.85	
% Daily Value		
Total Fat	1.92g	3%
Saturated Fat	0.26g	1%
Cholesterol	0mg	0%
Sodium	6.29mg	<1%
Potassium	193.29mg	6%
Total Carbohydrates	2.57g	<1%
Fiber	1.64g	7%
Sugar	0.93g	
Protein	0.96g	2%

Pumpkin Pie Spice Butter

This is so amazing and delicious- either on quinoa toast in the morning or just out of the jar! The 1.5 combination of maple sweetness and creamy pumpkin- it is like eating pumpkin pie...for breakfast!! *Makes over 1 cup of pumpkin butter*

Ingredients

- 1 cup of pumpkin puree
- 1/8 cup of water
- ¼ cup of maple syrup
- 1.5 teaspoons of pumpkin pie spice
- Dash of sea salt

Directions

Combine all of the above ingredients in a saucepan. Cook over medium heat, stirring constantly until the mixture thickens and becomes dark brown (Approximately 30 minutes).

☑ Smart Facts

With 7384 mg per 100 g, it is one of the vegetables in the Cucurbitaceae family featuring highest levels of vitamin-A, providing about 246% of RDA. Vitamin A is a powerful natural anti-oxidant and is required by the body for maintaining the integrity of skin and mucus membranes. It is also an essential vitamin for good visual sight. Research studies suggest that natural foods rich in vitamin A help a body protects against lung and oral cavity cancers.

☑ Nutritional Analysis

Amount Per Serving

Calories	50.35
Total Fat	0.19g
Saturated Fat	0.09g
Cholesterol	0mg
Sodium	3.62mg
Potassium	114.35mg
Total Carbohydrates	12.6g
Fiber	1.25g
Sugar	9.37g
Protein	0.47g

Warming Southwestern Black Bean Dip

I find this to be a great treat to welcome last minute visitors on a cold day; so easy and quick to make. The blend of fresh lime juice, coriander and cumin make an excellent filling in a gluten-free wrap topped with avocado and salsa for a quick and healthy meal.

Serves 10

Ingredients

- 1 large onion, chopped
- 1-2 cloves garlic, chopped
- 1 can black beans (19 oz.), drained and rinsed
- 2 cups chopped tomatoes
- 2 Tablespoons chilli powder
- 1 Tablespoon ground cumin
- ¾ cup chopped cilantro
- Juice of 1 lime

Directions

Gently cook onion and garlic in a lightly oiled pan, for 4 min. Add beans, tomatoes, chilli powder and cumin and simmer for 5-7 min. Mash with a potato masher remove from heat. Stir in cilantro and lime juice. Serve with chips or crackers.

☑ Smart Facts

Considering that black beans contain at least 8 different flavonoids with enormous antioxidant potential, and their high content of phytochemicals, it's hardly surprising that studies have connected black bean consumption with reduced risk of certain cancers. Recent studies have suggested considerable effectiveness against colon adenoma, a non-cancerous tumor that can progress into colon cancer.

RECIPE HIGHLIGHTS

* Easy to Make
* High in Fiber
* Low Glycemic
* No Added Sugar
* Vegetarian
* Vegan
* Dairy Free
* Diabetic Friendly

☑ Nutritional Analysis

Amount Per Serving	
Calories	56.12
Total Fat	0.64g
Saturated Fat	0.11g
Cholesterol	0mg
Sodium	81.69mg
Potassium	261.06mg
Total Carbohydrates	10.81g
Fiber	3.76g
Sugar	1.71g
Protein	3.18g

Spicy Spaghetti Squash

A spicy twist on a nutrient dense vegetable! My mother used to serve this vegetable to me when I was young and would tell me it was like nature's own pasta! This is a fun veggie to prepare for children because the strings do look like noodles! *Serves 8*

Ingredients

- 1 spaghetti squash, halved, seeds removed
- 1 teaspoon of chili powder
- 1 tablespoon of pure maple syrup
- 2 teaspoons of butter or coconut oil
- Sea salt and pepper to taste

Directions

Preheat oven to 400°F.

Place spaghetti squash, cut side down on a lightly greased baking pan. Bake squash until tender, 45-60 minutes. When cooked, remove the flesh from the squash using a fork. The squash will separate into "threads of pasta".

Add the butter, maple syrup and chili powder to the squash and toss gently.

Season with sea salt and pepper to taste.

☑ Smart Facts

Did you know that spaghetti squash contains calcium, iron, vitamin C and several B vitamins that strengthen the immune system?

RECIPE HIGHLIGHTS

* Easy to Make
* Egg Free
* Low Glycemic
* No Added Refined Sugars
* Vegetarian and Vegan

☑ Nutritional Analysis

Amount Per Serving	
Calories	95.06
Calories From Fat	19.05
Total Fat	2.18 g
Saturated Fat	1.27 g
Cholesterol	5.09 mg
Sodium	26.25 mg
Potassium	516.02 mg
Total Carbohydrates	20.08 g
Fibre	3.02 g
Sugar	6.1 g
Protein	1.5 g

(The 10% Rule) Desserts

Life always tastes better with a little sweetness in it! These desserts fall into my 10% guideline. 90% of the time—eat healthy. Only 10%? Life is short, eat dessert first.

Each dessert or sweet treat is created with only whole sweeteners and whole grains. White sugar is never used.

List of recipes:

- Anna Banana Bread
- Best Apple Pie with Roasted Almond Crust
- Cardamom Pecan Crisps
- Chocolate Banana Whole Grain Cookies
- Dark Chocolate Covered Bananas with Roasted Almonds
- Decadent Chocolate Pudding
- Decadent Dark Chocolate Pecan Bark
- Double Fudge Brownie
- High Fibre Peanut Butter Dark Chocalate Chip Cookies
- Paula's Powerful Date Square Cookies
- Chocolate Chip Cookies
- Chocolate Tempeh Cake

- Famous Energy Cookies
- Almond Shortbread Cookie
- Deep Dark Chocolate Zucchini Cake
- Pecan Maple Date Scones
- Perfect Gluten-Free Pastry

Anna Banana Bread

This banana bread is dedicated to my beautiful friend, Anne. I got the idea of this bread from the vegan banana bread that we both share (with butter on top!) when we go for a green tea at Bridgehead. It is sweet and moist and oh so yummy! The dates add richness without all of the added fat in regular banana bread!
Serves 12

Ingredients

- 2 cups of gluten-free all purpose flour mix OR whole wheat, kamut or spelt flour if not gluten sensitive
- 2 teaspoons of baking soda
- 1 teaspoon of gluten-free baking powder
- ½ teaspoon of sea salt
- 5 very ripe bananas, mashed
- ½ cup of pure maple syrup
- 1 teaspoon of vanilla extract
- ¾ cup of almond milk or cow's milk
- ¾ cup of chopped dates

Directions

Preheat oven to 350°F.

Mix all dry ingredients in a bowl. In another bowl, mash bananas, add maple syrup and vanilla and mix until incorporated. Gradually add in milk, mixing well. Add dry ingredients to the blended wet ingredients in three stages, blending well after each addition until the dry ingredients are completely incorporated. Add in chopped dates, mix well.

Pour into pre-greased loaf pan. Bake for 40-50 minutes or until toothpick comes out clean.

☑ Smart Facts

The Native Americans were the first to recognize the sap from maple trees as a source of energy and nutrition. They would use their tomahawks to make V-shaped incisions in the trees. Then, they would insert reeds or concave pieces of bark into the opening to run the sap into buckets made from birch bark. Studies have shown that maple syrup is a great source of antioxidants and trace vitamins and minerals!

RECIPE HIGHLIGHTS

* Dairy Free
* Easy to Make
* Egg Free
* No Added Refined Sugars
* Low Glycemic
* Vegetarian and Vegan (if using almond milk)

☑ Nutritional Analysis

Amount Per Serving

Calories	194.98
Total Fat	0.74 g
Saturated Fat	0.29 g
Cholesterol	1.22 mg
Sodium	315.97 mg
Potassium	322.13 mg
Total Carbohydrates	45.37 g
Fibre	2.74 g
Sugar	21.92 g
Protein	3.47 g

Best Apple Pie with Roasted Almond Crust

This apple pie is absolutely amazing and I have yet to have someone dislike it! The apples, cinnamon and almonds combine to make a perfect fall treat. *Serves 8*

Ingredients

Filling:

- 6-8 large apples, peeled, cored and sliced
- ½ cup of golden raisins
- 1-2 tablespoons of tapioca starch
- ¼ teaspoon of sea salt
- 2 teaspoons of cinnamon
- ½ cup of honey or maple syrup

Nut Crust:

- 4 tablespoons of coconut oil
- 4 tablespoons of honey or maple syrup
- ½ cup of brown rice flour
- 1 teaspoons of cinnamon
- 1½ cups of ground almonds

Directions

Preheat oven to 350°F.

Simmer apples and raisins with ¼ cup of water for 8-10 minutes until tender. Drain water from apples, but reserve in a small saucepan. Add cornstarch to reserved water plus an additional 1-2 tablespoons of water and heat until desired thickness is reached. Add simmered apples, raisins, honey/maple syrup and cinnamon to the thickened sauce.

For Crust: In a large bowl, combine coconut oil, honey/maple syrup, brown rice flour, cinnamon and ground almonds. Mix together using a pastry blender until the mixture resembles coarse meal. Pat ingredients into a 9-inch pie pan. Bake piecrust for 3-5 minutes at 350°F.
Cool for 5-10 minutes. Pour apple mixture into the crust. Bake for an additional 40 minutes at 250°F.

Serve warm.

☑ Smart Facts

An apple a day really does keep the doctor away. Apples help to detoxify metals from the body, protect against heart disease, lower blood cholesterol and blood pressure and help stabilize blood sugar.

This recipe is wonderful with any apple from your local farmers' market. My favorite is the "Honey Crisp" apple.

RECIPE HIGHLIGHTS
* Dairy Free
* Egg Free
* Vegetarian and Vegan
* High in Fibre
* No Added Refined Sugars

☑ Nutritional Analysis

Amount Per Serving

Calories	258.45
Total Fat	10.98 g
Saturated Fat	0.88 g
Cholesterol	0 mg
Sodium	42.58 mg
Potassium	313.39 mg
Total Carbohydrates	39.27 g
Fibre	4.05 g
Sugar	25.06 g
Protein	4.75 g

Cardamom Pecan Crisps

The pecans add a rich texture along with the cardamom and cinnamon to give a crunchy, healthy cookie. Almost "shortbread" like it is perfect with a cup of green chai tea. The warm and lemon-musky overtones of cardamom combine well with sweet maple in this gluten-free cookie. *Makes 36 cookies*

Ingredients

- 2 cups of brown rice flour
- 2 cups of pecan halves, finely ground
- 2 teaspoons of cinnamon
- 1 teaspoon of ground cardamom
- 1 teaspoon of sea salt
- ¾ cup of coconut oil
- ¾ cup of pure maple syrup

Directions

Grease baking sheets and preheat oven to 350°F.

Mix together all dry ingredients in a bowl. In a separate bowl, whisk together oil and maple syrup until emulsified.

Pour the liquid ingredients into the dry ingredients whisking continuously until all of the dry ingredients have been incorporated.

Using a tablespoon, place batter on parchment-lined baking sheet and flatten with a wet fork until each crisp is fairly thin.

Bake in preheated oven for 20 minutes until they are golden brown and crisp. Remove from oven and allow to cool slightly before removing them from the pan. Cool completely on cooling rack, stacking cookies in a single layer to prevent sticking.

☑ Smart Facts

From the ginger family, cardamom is quite the little nutritional powerhouse. Cardamom is rich in calcium, potassium, phosphorus and magnesium. It also contains moderate amounts of iron, sodium and manganese.

Cardamom is used to treat teeth and gum infections, digestive disorders, dysentery, constipation, congestion of lungs and throat problems.

RECIPE HIGHLIGHTS

* Simple and Quick
* Dairy Free
* Egg Free
* No Added Refined sugars
* Vegetarian and Vegan

☑ Nutritional Analysis

Amount Per Serving

Calories	131.01
Total Fat	9.17 g
Saturated Fat	4.35 g
Cholesterol	0 mg
Sodium	39.3 mg
Potassium	65.12 mg
Total Carbohydrates	12.22 g
Fibre	1.08 g
Sugar	4.31 g
Protein	1.2 g

Chocolate Banana Whole Grain Cookies

This is the perfect pre and post workout snack. The combination of complex carbohydrates, protein and healthy fat is the perfect replenishment for tired muscles.
Makes 36 cookies

Ingredients

- 3 large ripe bananas, mashed, (about 1½ cups)
- 1 teaspoon of vanilla extract
- ¼ cup of coconut oil or butter
- 2 cups of gluten-free, quick cooking rolled oats
- ⅔ cup of ground almonds
- ⅓ cup of unsweetened, shredded coconut
- 2 teaspoons of cinnamon
- ½ teaspoon of fine grain sea salt
- 1 teaspoon of gluten-free baking powder
- 7 ounces of dark chocolate chopped or about 1 cup of dark chocolate chips

Directions

Preheat oven to 350°F.

In a large bowl, combine the bananas, vanilla extract, and oil or butter. Set aside.

In a separate bowl, combine the oats, ground almonds, shredded coconut, cinnamon, sea salt and baking powder. Add the dry ingredients to the wet ingredients and stir until combined. Fold in the chocolate chunks or chips.

Using a teaspoon, drop the dough into small rounds on a parchment-lined baking sheet, about an inch apart.

Bake for 12-14 minutes. Allow cookies to cool on the pan before transferring to a rack to cool completely.

☑ Smart Facts

Did you know that coconut oil is a heart healthy fat that stimulates the metabolism by stimulating the thyroid?

The cinnamon in these cookies is also very beneficial in balancing the blood sugar after a workout and the banana helps to replace lost potassium and electrolytes lost during intense physical activity.

Enjoy just the right amount of chocolate.

RECIPE HIGHLIGHTS

* Simple and Quick
* Egg free
* High in Fibre
* No Added Refined Sugars
* Vegetarian and Vegan

☑ Nutritional Analysis

Amount Per Serving	
Calories	98.21
Total Fat	6.3 g
Saturated Fat	2.44 g
Cholesterol	0 mg
Sodium	43.81 mg
Potassium	93.34 mg
Total Carbohydrates	10.32 g
Fibre	1.85 g
Sugar	1.83 g
Protein	1.72 g

Decadent Chocolate Pudding

I often demo this recipe at my cooking classes and always enjoy the enthusiastic responses I receive about how delicious and creamy this is. No one will ever guess that there is avocado in it! *Serves 8*

Ingredients

- 4 ounces of dark 70% chocolate
- 3 ripe avocados, diced
- ½ cup of maple syrup
- 2 teaspoons of vanilla extract
- 2 tablespoons of almond, hemp or rice milk
- ½ cup of softened dates
- ½ ripe banana
- Pinch of sea salt
- Chopped toasted almonds for garnish

Directions

Melt the chocolate gently on low heat in a small saucepan.

Place avocado, maple syrup, dates, vanilla, banana and sea salt into a food processor and purée. Add the melted chocolate and purée until completely incorporated.

Add the milk one tablespoon at a time and continue to purée to a creamy consistency.

Serve in a martini glass and garnish with chopped almonds or fresh cherries.

☑ Smart Facts

Often times people buy avocados that are not ripe enough. You can tell an avocado is ripe when it is just soft to the touch. If the avocados are still hard, store your avocados beside your bananas. The gases released from the bananas can ripen an avocado almost overnight.

RECIPE HIGHLIGHTS
* Simple and Quick
* Vegetarian and Vegan
* Egg Free
* No Added Refined Sugars

☑ Nutritional Analysis

Amount Per Serving	
Calories	174.16
Total Fat	8.84 g
Saturated Fat	2.17 g
Cholesterol	0 mg
Sodium	30.02 mg
Potassium	320.69 mg
Total Carbohydrates	25.61 g
Fibre	4.24 g
Sugar	15.25 g
Protein	1.41 g

Decadent Dark Chocolate Pecan Bark

Decadent is the only word to describe this one! I love to box this chocolate decadence in festive containers and give it as a Christmas gift.
Serves 12

Ingredients

- 1 teaspoon of butter
- 1 cup of pecan pieces
- 1 tablespoon of maple syrup
- 1 cup of dark chocolate
- 1 teaspoon of vanilla extract
- Pinch of sea salt

Directions

Melt butter over medium high heat in a frying pan. Add pecans and maple syrup stirring constantly until syrup starts to boil and pecans become coated. Remove pan from heat and set aside.

Melt chocolate in a double boiler over low heat. Add vanilla, sea salt and candied pecans and mix thoroughly.

Pour chocolate mixture onto a parchment-lined baking pan and spread out in a thin layer with a spatula.

Transfer pan to fridge and allow mixture to set for 1 hour.

Once set, break or cut into bite size pieces.

☑ Smart Facts

I often will melt 1 square of white chocolate and add to the top of dark chocolate while it is still warm for the added "swirling" effect.

Pecans are a native North American member of the hickory family. Pecans contain more than 19 vitamins and minerals—including vitamin A, vitamin E, potassium, folic acid, calcium, magnesium, phosphorus, several B vitamins and zinc.

RECIPE HIGHLIGHTS

* Simple and Quick
* Egg Free
* Vegetarian
* High in Antioxidants
* Absolutely Decadent

☑ Nutritional Analysis

Amount Per Serving

Calories	138.01
Total Fat	11.06 g
Saturated Fat	3.25 g
Cholesterol	0.85 mg
Sodium	3.99 mg
Potassium	41.25 mg
Total Carbohydrates	11.3 g
Fibre	1.7 g
Sugar	1.4 g
Protein	1.42 g

Double Fudge Brownie

This recipe comes out of a funny story as I was trying to convince my best friend, Anne that black beans could be used in a chocolate muffin or baked good recipe. It made sense to me ... I was determined to make this happen. And wow! Here it is; one of my favourite, double chocolate recipes yet! *Makes 12 brownies*

Ingredients

- 1 (19-ounce/540-millilitre) can of black beans, rinsed
- 3 eggs
- ½ cup of unsweetened cocoa
- ½ cup of butter or coconut oil
- ¾ cup of sucanat
- ½ cup of dark 70% chocolate chips
- 1 tablespoon of vanilla extract
- ⅔ cup of walnuts.

Directions

Preheat oven to 350°F.

Add all ingredients, except walnuts, to a food processor and purée.

Stir in walnuts.

Add brownie batter to a pre-greased 8 x 8 inch baking pan.

Bake for 30 minutes or until toothpick comes out clean.

Serve with melted dark chocolate, fresh mango and coconut milk ice cream.

☑ Smart Facts

Black beans are an excellent source of fibre and protein.

Black Beans have more antioxidant activity, gram for gram, than other beans. In general, darker colored seed coats were associated with higher levels of flavonoids, and therefore higher antioxidant activity, says lead investigator Clifford W. Beninger, Ph.D., a research associate at the University of Guelph in Ontario, Canada.

RECIPE HIGHLIGHTS

* Simple and Quick
* Low Glycemic
* No added Refined Sugars
* Vegetarian
* High in Fibre
* High in Protein

☑ Nutritional Analysis

Amount Per Serving	
Calories	253.71
Total Fat	15.86 g
Saturated Fat	7.21 g
Cholesterol	73.21 mg
Sodium	130.24 mg
Potassium	198.53 mg
Total Carbohydrates	26.1 g
Fibre	3.91 g
Sugar	13.81 g
Protein	5.56 g

High Fibre Peanut Butter Dark Chocolate Chip Cookies

I first made these for my teen girl's fitness class when they asked me to find a healthy recipe with peanut butter and chocolate—this was the result and they have been gobbled up by many!
Serves 12-16

Ingredients

- 1 cup natural crunchy peanut butter
- 1 cup honey or pure maple syrup
- 1 egg
- ¾ cup gluten-free flour blend
- 1 teaspoon vanilla extract
- ½ teaspoon of baking powder
- ½ teaspoon of gluten-free baking soda
- ½ teaspoon of sea salt
- 1½ cups quick cooking gluten-free oats
- ½ cup dark 70% cocoa chocolate chips (heaping)

Directions

Preheat oven to 375°F.

In a large bowl, cream together peanut butter, egg, vanilla extract, and honey until smooth.

Combine the gluten-free flour, baking soda, baking powder, oats, chocolate chips, and sea salt and stir into the creamed mixture.

Drop by tablespoonfuls onto a cookie sheet. Bake for 8-10 minutes. Allow cookies to cool for 5 minutes on baking sheet before removing to cool completely.

☑ Smart Facts

The unsaturated fat content in peanut butter helps reduce the risk of heart disease by 25% (if you eat 1 ounce per day), its rich folate and niacin (vitamin B3) content helps increase the HDL (good cholesterol) level by as much as 30%, all the while being a very good source of protein!

RECIPE HIGHLIGHTS

* Simple and Quick
* No Added Refined Sugars
* High in Fibre
* High in Protein

☑ Nutritional Analysis

Amount Per Serving

Calories	237.81
Total Fat	10.54 g
Saturated Fat	2.43 g
Cholesterol	13.22 mg
Sodium	106.59 mg
Potassium	186.02 mg
Total Carbohydrates	33.6 g
Fibre	3.1 g
Sugar	18.91 g
Protein	6.33 g

Paula's Powerful Date Square Cookies

My friend Paula is one of the most fit instructors I know in the City of Ottawa! We go to fitness conferences together and learn all kinds of new fitness moves to teach to our clients. Paula made these cookies for us as we needed a gluten-free pre and post workout snack that was yummy, full of protein and could keep us going all day during our fitness conferences.

Makes 24 cookies

Ingredients

- ½ cup of softened butter or coconut oil
- ⅓ cup of sucanat
- 1 egg
- ⅓ cup of ground almonds
- ⅓ cup of ground flaxseeds
- 1½ cups of gluten-free oats
- 2 cups of pitted and chopped dates

Directions

Preheat oven to 350°F.

Cream together butter/coconut oil, sucanat and egg. Add ground almonds, flaxseeds, oats and dates and form into small balls.

Place on parchment-lined cookie sheets and bake in the oven for 10 minutes. Remove from oven, allow to cool on baking sheets for 5 minutes, and then transfer to a wire rack to cool completely.

☑ Smart Facts

Dates have a natural sweetness that tastes like maple syrup or brown sugar! Dates are rich in minerals like calcium, potassium, manganese, copper and high in B vitamins and vitamin K.

RECIPE HIGHLIGHTS

* Simple and Quick
* Dairy Free (if using coconut oil)
* High in Fibre
* No Added Refined Sugars
* Vegetarian and Vegan (if using coconut oil)

☑ Nutritional Analysis

Amount Per Serving	
Calories	120.93
Total Fat	5.44 g
Saturated Fat	2.63 g
Cholesterol	18.98 mg
Sodium	31.63 mg
Potassium	137.9 mg
Total Carbohydrates	17.94 g
Fibre	1.92 g
Sugar	12.52 g
Protein	1.76 g

Good Old Fashioned Chocolate Chip Cookies...with a twist

Of course, in the Smart kitchen a chocolate chip cookie isn't just a cookie...it is a way to make healthy food delicious.

The twist? Chickpeas! Yes you read right-chickpeas...This melt in your mouth cookie made with the humble bean.

Makes 16-18 amazing cookies

Ingredients

- 1 can (15 ounce can) chick peas, drained
- ½ cup of natural peanut, almond or cashew butter
- ½ cup of Sucanat or coconut sugar
- 1 Tablespoon of vanilla extract
- 1/8 tsp sea salt
- ½ teaspoon gluten-free baking powder
- ¾ cups dark chocolate chips

Directions

Preheat oven to 350 F

Add all ingredients except chocolate chips into a blender and puree.

Add in chocolate chips and stir.

Scoop 1 inch thick balls onto a greased cookie sheet.

Flatten cookies with a fork

Bake for 15-20 minutes, or until chocolate chips are melting

Remove from oven and let cool.

RECIPE HIGHLIGHTS
* Dairy Free
* Egg Free
* No Added Refined Sugars

☑ Nutritional Analysis

Amount Per Serving	
Calories	99
Total Fat	6.2g
Cholesterol	0mg
Sodium	32mg
Potassium	52.8mg
Carbohydrates	11.5g
Fiber	<1g
Sugar	5.9g
Protein	1.3g

High Protein Tempeh Chocolate Cake

This cake is loaded in protein from tempeh and almond butter- it is delicious even for breakfast! *Serves 12*

Ingredients

- 3 Tablespoons coconut oil
- 8 ounce crumbled plain tempeh
- 1 ½ cups coconut sugar or Sucanat
- 2 cups plain, unsweetened almond milk
- 1 Tablespoon vanilla extract
- ¼ cup almond butter
- ½ teaspoon sea salt
- ½ cup unsweetened apple sauce
- 2 cups all-purpose gluten-free flour blend and 3 Tablespoons of ground flax
- 2/3 cups unsweetened cocoa powder
- 2½ teaspoons gluten-free baking powder
- ¾ cup dairy- free chocolate chips or dark chocolate chips if not dairy intolerant

Topping

- Combine well 1 cup fruit juice sweetened raspberry fruit puree with ¾ cup of cocoa powder

Directions

Preheat oven to 350 degrees.

Add oil to a medium pan and fry tempeh until golden. Add coconut sugar/Sucanat and stir until well combined and dissolved.

Combine all of the wet ingredients in a food processor until well combined.

Stir dry ingredients together. Fold wet ingredients in to dry ingredients.

Grease a 9 by 9 inch pan with coconut oil. Pour the mixture into pan, and bake in the oven for 35 minutes.

☑ Smart Facts

Tempeh is made from cooked and slightly fermented soybeans and formed into a patty, similar to a very firm veggie burger. It is VERY high in protein and because it is fermented- it is a much healthier soy alternative than tofu. You can find tempeh in your local health food store.

RECIPE HIGHLIGHTS

* Dairy Free
* Egg Free
* Diabetic Friendly
* Gluten and Wheat Free
* No Added Refined Sugars
* Vegetarian and Vegan
* High in Protein

☑ Nutritional Analysis

Amount Per Serving		
Calories	232	321.8
Calories From Fat (30%)		95.06
% Daily Value		
Total Fat	11.38g	18%
Saturated Fat	4.85g	24%
Cholesterol	0mg	0%
Sodium	171.66mg	7%
Potassium	260.38mg	7%
Total Carbohydrates	55.28g	18%
Fiber	5.41g	22%
Sugar	15.75g	
Protein	9.01g	14%

Remove from oven and allow to cool. When completely cooled, add the raspberry topping.

Kathy's Famous Energy Cookies

These cookies are yummy and very high in calcium due to the sesame seeds and tahini. One cookie has more calcium than 1.5 cups of milk- and it is a calcium that is more absorbable. These cookies are a PERFECT and delicious way to get in that bone building calcium without dairy.

Ingredients

- 2 cups of brown rice flour
- 1 cup of ground almonds
- ½ cup ground pecans
- 1 cup of sesame seeds
- 1 teaspoon of sea salt
- 2 teaspoons of cinnamon
- 1 Tablespoon of vanilla extract
- ½-¾ cup tahini (ground sesame paste)
- ¾-1 cup pure maple syrup
- Apple Butter (can be found in a bulk food/ health food store)

Directions

Add all dry ingredients in a large bowl and mix thoroughly. Add the tahini and maple syrup and mix thoroughly. Massage cookie mixture with hands to release the oils of the ground nuts until mixture sticks together to form a ball. If after massage the dough does not form a ball, add a small amount of water. Take cookie mixture and spoon out with an ice cream scoop into ball on a non-stick cookie pan. Flatten ball with a fork and form a "thumbprint" in the middle of cookie and fill with apple butter.

Bake at 350 F for 10-12 minutes or until golden brown.

☑ Smart Facts

RECIPE HIGHLIGHTS

- * Easy to Make
- * Egg Free
- * Dairy Free
- * Gluten and Wheat Free
- * High in Calcium
- * Low Glycemic
- * No Added Refined Sugars
- * Vegetarian/ Vegan

☑ Nutritional Analysis

Amount Per Serving	
Calories	281.49
Total Fat	14.07g
Saturated Fat	1.68g
Cholesterol	0mg
Sodium	128.47mg
Potassium	227.5mg
Total Carbohydrates	35.17g
Fiber	4.02g
Sugar	12.77g
Protein	5.98g

Perfect Gluten Free Pastry

... just like my grandmamma used to make! This is so so easy... and perfect every time. This recipe can be used for any type of pie. Perfect pastry - every time! *Makes 6 shells*

Ingredients

- 5½ cups all-purpose gluten-free flour blend (I like Bob's of Redmill)
- 2 teaspoons of sea salt
- 1 Tablespoon of guar gum + 1 Tablespoon of psyllium husks
- 1 lb. of coconut oil or lard
- 1 Tablespoon of white vinegar
- 1 egg, lightly beaten
- Ice cold water

Directions

Mix together flour, sea salt, guar gum and psyllium. Cut in coconut oil or lard with pastry blender until mixture resembles coarse oatmeal.

In a 1-cup measure, combine vinegar and egg. Add enough cold water to make one cup. Gradually stir liquid into flour mixture. Add only enough liquid to make dough cling together. Gather into a ball and make six portions. Each ball is one shell.

Refrigerate for 2 hours (do not skip this step)

Roll out pie dough on a floured surface with gluten-free flour blend.

Grandmama's tip?

Do NOT overwork the pastry...

☑ Smart Facts

RECIPE HIGHLIGHTS
* Gluten-Free
* Easy to Make
* Dairy Free
* No Added Refined Sugars
* No White Rice Flours

☑ Nutritional Analysis

Ok- I debated this back and forth and decided against doing the calories for a pastry or pie crust.

My grandmamma said that pie calories don't count and to go for a walk after....

I am going to heed that advice and realize that sometimes....it is better to not know!

Almond Shortbread Cookies

Shortbreads are one of my favourite cookies. Scottish in origin, this rich, tender and crumbly cookie is served every Christmas in the Smart home. I have smartened up the traditional shortbread cookie of flour, butter and sugar to using ground almonds and healthy sweeteners to make decadence and health come together- in shortbread style! *Makes 36 cookies*

Ingredients

- 2 cups ground almonds
- 1 ½ cups brown rice flour
- 1/3 cup organic sucanat or coconut sugar
- 1 egg beaten
- ½ cup coconut oil
- 1/3 cup agave nectar or coconut nectar
- 1 teaspoon almond extract
- 1/3 cup whole raw almonds

Directions

Preheat oven to 325 degrees F.

Lightly grease a cookie sheet. Combine ground almonds, rice flour and sucanat in a large bowl. Blend egg, butter, agave nectar, and almond extract in a separate bowl. Add dry ingredients to wet ½ cup at a time until well blended,

Roll dough into small, round balls, flatten slightly with fingers or a fork and then press a whole almond into the center of each cookie

Place cookies on a cookie sheet and bake for 10 to 12 minutes.

☑ Smart Facts

A high-fat food that's good for your health? That's not an oxymoron, its almonds. Almonds are high in monounsaturated fats, the same type of health-promoting fats as are found in olive oil, which have been associated with reduced risk of heart disease.

RECIPE HIGHLIGHTS

* Dairy free
* Gluten-Free
* Vegetarian
* No Added Refined Sugars
* Low Glycemic
* Diabetic Friendly

☑ Nutritional Analysis

Amount Per Serving
Serving size: 1/36 of a recipe (19 grams).

Calories	86.03
Total Fat	4.97g
Saturated Fat	0.52g
Cholesterol	6.3mg
Sodium	4.26mg
Potassium	87.04mg
Total Carbohydrates	8.71g
Fiber	1.31g
Sugar	2.45g
Protein	2.54g

Deep Dark Chocolate Zucchini Cake

Serves 16

Ingredients

- ½ cup coconut oil or butter at room temperature
- ¼ cup unsweetened apple sauce
- 1¼ cup of coconut sugar or sucanat
- 2 large eggs (or if you want a vegan version use 4 Tablespoons of ground flax + 4 Tablespoons of water to substitute)
- 2 teaspoons of vanilla
- 1 teaspoon of orange zest (grated orange peel)
- 1 cup plain Greek yogurt (or unsweetened apple sauce if dairy intolerant)
- 2 cups grated unpeeled zucchini
- 2 ¼ cups all purpose gluten-free flour
- ¾ cup unsweetened cocoa
- 1 teaspoon gluten-free baking powder
- 1 teaspoon baking soda
- ½ teaspoon sea salt
- ¾ cup chopped walnuts or chocolate chips, or both

Deep Dark Vegan Frosting

- 1 cup dark chocolate chips
- ½ cup coconut oil
- 3 tablespoons maple syrup
- 1 tablespoon vanilla extract
- pinch sea salt

Directions

Preheat oven to 325°F

Pre grease a baking pan with coconut oil.

In a large bowl, beat the butter, applesauce and sugar on high speed with an electric mixer for 2-3 minutes, until thick. Stir in the eggs, vanilla, zest, yogurt and zucchini.

☑ Nutritional Analysis

Amount Per Serving
Serving size: 1/16 of a recipe (126 grams). Percent daily values based on the Reference Daily Intake (RDI) for a 2000 calorie diet. Nutrition information calculated from recipe ingredients

Calories		417.1
Calories From Fat (50%)		206.65
% Daily Value		
Total Fat	24.49g	38%
Saturated Fat	15.91g	80%
Cholesterol	26.44mg	9%
Sodium	195.01mg	8%
Potassium	147.42mg	4%
Total Carbohydrates	50.01g	17%
Fiber	4.79g	19%
Sugar	22.66g	
Protein	6.57g	13%

Combine all dry ingredients. Add the dry ingredients by the cup full into the wet ingredients until well combined.

Bake for 1 hour or until a toothpick comes out clean. Serve with your favorite icing.

Deep Dark Vegan Frosting

In a small saucepan over very low heat, melt chocolate and coconut oil.

Stir in maple syrup, vanilla and salt.

Place frosting in freezer for 20 minutes to chill and thicken.

Remove from freezer and whip frosting with a hand blender until it is fluffy and frosting looking. Enjoy!

Pecan Maple Date Scones

Boy oh boy...the smell of these coming out of the oven is heaven on earth. The rich texture of ground almonds and pecans and the natural sweetness of dates and maple syrup...a favorite to wake up to!! *Makes 16 scones*

Ingredients

- 1/ 2 cup ground pecans
- 2 cups ground almonds
- ½ cup pecan halves + ½ cup raisins or chopped dates
- 1/ 2 teaspoon each of sea salt, baking soda
- 1/3 cup of melted coconut oil + 1/3 cup of maple syrup
- 2 eggs

Directions

Preheat the oven to 350 degrees F.

Pre grease a baking sheet.

In a large bowl combine all the dry ingredients.

In a large bowl whisk together all wet ingredients.

Fold dry ingredients into wet by the ½ cup and blend.

Drop the batter by 2 Tablespoons 2 inches apart onto prepared baking sheets.

Bake for 12-17 minutes and enjoy heaven!

☑ Smart Facts

RECIPE HIGHLIGHTS

* Gluten and Wheat Free
* Dairy Free
* No Added Refined Sugars
* High in Protein

☑ Nutritional Analysis

Amount Per Serving
Serving size: 1/16 of a recipe (42 grams). Percent daily values based on the Reference Daily Intake (RDI) for a 2000 calorie diet. Nutrition information calculated from recipe ingredients.

Calories		196.62
Calories From Fat (69%)		135.18
% Daily Value		
Total Fat	15.97g	25%
Saturated Fat	4.99g	25%
Cholesterol	26.44mg	9%
Sodium	107.66mg	4%
Potassium	170.19mg	5%
Total Carbohydrates	12.24g	4%
Fiber	2.55g	10%
Sugar	8.29g	
Protein	4.07g	8%

Dark Chocolate Covered Bananas with Roasted Almonds

I have been dairy intolerant since I was 4 years old. My mother would make this dairy free dessert for me when my best friend Kelly would come over to play. These soon became a neighbourhood hit and my girlfriends and I would go digging in the freezer for these every play date along with frozen strawberries. *Serves 2*

Ingredients

- 2 wooden popsicle sticks
- 1 large ripe banana, halved
- ½ cup of dark chocolate chips or chocolate bar (at least 70% cocoa), melted
- 2 tablespoons of crushed, roasted almonds or almond slivers

Directions

Insert popsicle sticks into the bottoms of the 2 banana halves.

Melt the chocolate over low heat. Spread crushed almonds on a plate.

Dip the bananas into the melted chocolate, covering the entire surface area of the banana halves.

Roll the chocolate-coated banana in the almonds until lightly coated.

Lie chocolate covered bananas on a plate and freeze for 3-4 hours.

☑ **Smart Facts**

Chocolate is derived from plants, which means it contains many of the health benefits from antioxidants like dark, green vegetables. These antioxidants protect the body from damaging free radicals that can cause various health problems. Dark chocolate contains 8 times more antioxidants than strawberries!

RECIPE HIGHLIGHTS

- * Simple and Quick
- * Egg Free
- * No Added Refined Sugars
- * Vegetarian and Vegan

☑ **Nutritional Analysis**

Amount Per Serving

Calories	148.84
Calories From Fat	65.94
Total Fat	7.76 g
Saturated Fat	3.35 g
Cholesterol	0 mg
Sodium	5.36 mg
Potassium	160.3 mg
Total Carbohydrates	21.45 g
Fibre	2.57 g
Sugar	4.55 g
Protein	1.476 g

Recipe Highlight Terms

Food allergies and intolerances are becoming more widespread than ever before. With all of my recipes I have included a handy "Recipe Highlights" chart which indicates the particular characteristics of each recipe as it relates to diet. This includes indicating if a recipe is void of certain allergens or if it is appropriate for particular diets etc.

The following list provides a definition of what each recipe highlight means.

Dairy Free

This recipe is void of dairy products including the enzyme "lactose" and the milk protein "casein".

Diabetic Friendly

This recipe is higher in protein and lower in complex carbohydrates making it a safe choice for the insulin resistant, hypoglycemic or diabetic.

Simple and Quick

This recipe is especially easy and quick to make.

Egg Free

This recipe is void of any egg products.

High in...

This indicates that a specific recipe is particularly high in a particular nutrient.

Low Glycemic

The glycemic index (GI) is a rating of a carbohydrate according to how quickly it raises your blood sugar level as they are broken down and digested. The more refined a carbohydrate, the higher it rates on the glycemic index. High glycemic foods trigger a spike and then a drop in blood sugar. This quick burst of energy is then followed by a sudden crash of energy leaving the individual craving their next shot of sugar or caffeine. Low glycemic foods are higher in fibre and break down slower in your blood stream, thus giving your body a constant, steady supply of sustained energy.

NO Added Refined Sugars

This recipe is free from any added refined sugar in the form of glucose, sucrose, dextrose, corn syrup, invert sugar, turbinado, caramel and brown sugar. When sweeteners are called for in a recipe, natural, unrefined sweeteners such as pure maple syrup, sucanat, agave nectar, brown rice syrup and honey are used instead.

Vegan

This recipe does not use any animal protein or products derived from an animal including eggs, honey, dairy or gelatin.

Vegetarian

This recipe is free of any animal protein.

Commonly Used Ingredients

Coconut Oil

For years many believed that coconut oil was very dangerous and unhealthy for you. The negative research done on coconut oil in the past was the result of one study conducted four decades ago, using hydrogenated oil (which has been processed and altered from its original form), not on virgin coconut oil. Research shows that some saturated fat is in fact necessary for human health and modern research shows that the medium chain fatty acids (MCFA) help to increase metabolism and are more easily digested than fats found in other oils. Medium Chain Triglyceride Fats are processed directly in the liver and immediately converted into energy. As a result, there is less strain on the liver, pancreas and digestive system and these MCFA provide the body with a wonderful, quick source of energy. Coconut oil also has a higher smoking point than canola oil making it a much healthier alternative.

Maple Syrup

One ounce of maple syrup contains 46 percent of the daily value of manganese. Manganese is needed for healthy nerves, a healthy metabolism and blood sugar regulation. In my recipes, I use whole sweeteners full of nutrients instead of white sugar which is devoid of all nutrients. Be sure to purchase Grade B Maple as it contains a higher nutrient profile than Grade A, which is more processed, but has a lighter taste. Maple syrup is also high in potassium and calcium. Use in coffee, baked goods, as a glaze for meat or tofu and in teriyaki sauce. When substituting maple syrup in recipes, reduce your liquid slightly. Maple syrup is also available in crystals.

Whole Eggs

The cholesterol in eggs has very little effect on blood cholesterol levels in adults. Major clinical studies have shown that there is no relationship between egg consumption and an increased risk of heart attack or stroke. Stop throwing away your yolks. The yolk of the egg is where 90% of the nutrition comes from. You are short-changing yourself by throwing out the good stuff! The yolk contains ½ of the protein and amino acid profile.

Butter

For years butter had been falsely maligned and is now beginning to make a comeback as the healthy fat that it is. Butter contains many nutrients that protect against heart disease, including natural vitamins A, D and E, and lecithin, selenium and possibly iodine when soils are near the ocean. A Medical Research Council survey showed that men eating butter ran half the risk of developing heart disease as those using margarine. The short and medium chained fatty acids in butter have strong anti-tumor effects. Conjugated linoelic acid (CLA) in orange butter from grass-fed cows also gives excellent protection against cancer. Butter is a rich source of easily absorbed vitamin A needed for a wide range of functions from maintaining good vision to keeping the endocrine system in top shape. Butter also contains all the other fat-soluble vitamins D3, E and K2, which are often lacking in the modern industrial diet.

Honey

Honey is composed of sugars like glucose and fructose and minerals like magnesium, potassium, calcium, sodium chlorine, sulphur, iron and phosphate. Honey also contains vitamins B1, B2, C, B6, B5 and B3. I prefer to use honey over white sugar in my recipes. To substitue sugare, replace 1 cup of sugar with a generous ¾ cup of honey and use 2-4 tablespoons less of other liquid in the recipe. Because honey is more acidic than sugar, add a pinch of baking soda to neutralize the added acid. Honey will make the baked good brown faster, so reduce the cooking temperature by 25 degrees. Honey will make the baked good darker and denser than sugar while giving it a moister texture. Purchase raw, local honey to aide in adapting to pollen and preventing hay fever and for the beneficial enzymes usually destroyed during pasteurization.

Brown Rice Syrup

Brown Rice Syrup is a sweetener made by fermenting brown rice and boiling the resulting mixture until it becomes a sweet rich syrup. It is similar in texture to honey. Brown rice syrup is only 20% as sweet as sugar making it a sweetener that some diabetics can tolerate if eaten with protein. To substitute, use 1¼ cup rice syrup for one cup of sugar, using ¼ cup less of another liquid needed in the recipe. Brown rice syrup adds a caramel note to any recipe.

Agave Nectar

Organic Agave Nectar is a natural sweetener that is similar to honey. It is harvested from live cactii by the indigenous peoples of Mexico. Agave has a relatively low glycemic index due to its higher proportion of fructose and lower levels of glucose. To substitute use ¾ cup agave nectar per 1 cup of other sweetener. When substituting agave in recipes, reduce your liquid slightly, sometimes as much as 1/3 less. In comparison to some of the other natural sweeteners, agave nectar holds up well to heat and does not add a distinctive taste like other sweeteners—only a sweetness.

Coconut Flour

Coconut flour is made by drying pieces of coconut meat and grinding it into a fine powder. It is absolutely free of gluten. Interestingly it consists of 58% fibre, giving it the highest level of fibre on the flour market. Studies have found fibre to be beneficial in protecting against cardiovascular diseases, helping lower cholesterol, promoting good intestinal health and moderating blood sugar and insulin levels.

Ground Almonds

Almonds are a nutritional powerhouse that contain significant amounts of protein, calcium, fibre, magnesium, folic acid, potassium, and vitamin E. Research suggests that eating one ounce of almonds per day may lower LDL (bad cholesterol) because of their healthful monounsaturated fats. Their high levels of arginine have also been shown to help reduce the risk of coronary disease.

Brown Rice Flour

Brown rice flour is the most common of the gluten-free grains. It is an excellent source of protein, vitamin B and minerals such as magnesium and selenium. It is also very rich in fibre, about 26%, which has been shown to be beneficial in helping control blood sugar levels.

Sucanat

Sucanat is the short name for sugar cane natural. The granular form retains more minerals during processing than organic raw sugar. Sucanat is great in coffee and best in baked goods that produce a darker, richer color such as chocolate chip, oatmeal and gingerbread cookies. Sucanat has an almost molasses like taste adding a rich caramel undertone to any baked good.

In all recipes, local, organic ingredients are always preferred as not only do they taste better—they are better for the earth and for us all.

What is Gluten?

- Gluten is a protein found within the seeds or grains of wheat, rye, barley, spelt, kamut and triticale

- The proteins are loosely called "gluten", but gluten is made up of several subfractions of proteins

- Gluten acts as a rubbery kind of binder when liquid is added, and gives bread and wheat products their doughy texture

What is Gluten Intolerance?

Gluten intolerance (also commonly referred to as gluten sensitivity) takes place when a person cannot tolerate gluten. Any individual who has celiac disease is in essence gluten "intolerant/sensitive". Usually, the term "gluten intolerant" describes individuals who get symptoms when they eat gluten, and feel better on a gluten-free diet, but do not have celiac disease per se. Common symptoms of gluten intolerance/sensitivity include abdominal pain, fatigue, headaches and paresthesia, which refers to tingling of the extremities (Canadian Celiac Association, 2011).

Is wheat healthy for those who are not gluten intolerant?

- Modern wheat – the product of genetics research for increased yield conducted in the 1970s - is a source of the protein gliadin, which is an opiate. But this opiate does not make us "high"; gliadin is an appetite-stimulant. Many medical professionals now believe that it is not fat, but wheat that is causing the obesity epidemic in North America.

- Wheat increases blood sugar higher than 6 teaspoons of table sugar. Advice to "eat more healthy whole grains" is little better than being told to eat candy bars at every meal.

Printed with permission by Dr. William Davis, MD, 2012

What is Celiac Disease?

Villi in the Small Intestines

We now know that celiac disease was, and continues to be underestimated. Celiac disease was first described in 1888 by Dr. Samuel Gee, and reiterated by Dr. R.A. Gibbons, as a disease of malabsorption. In the 1930s, Dr. Dicke discovered that a wheat-free diet resulted in a full remission of symptoms. In 1950, a surgical device was developed to biopsy tissue samples from the small intestinal lining. It was this invention that led to redefining celiac disease during the 1960s.

Today more than 2 million North Americans suffer from celiac disease. When actively sought, celiac disease is found in approximately 1% of apparently healthy, symptom-free American adults, making it more than twice as common as inflammatory bowel disease. And those numbers are expected to rise.

Cases of celiac disease found in children are equally spread among males and females. In adults, however, twice as many women are diagnosed in comparison to men.

- Much of what we eat is absorbed through the surface of the small intestines via the villi

- Villi are small, finger like projections in the small intestine that increase the surface area of the small intestine

- Villi line the small intestines, and help increase the absorption area for nutrients

- In celiac disease, the small intestines become so damaged by gluten that villi become flat, and cannot do their job of absorbing nutrients. Therefore, many nutrient deficiencies can occur in the celiac individual

- Symptoms of celiac disease include muscle soreness, joint pain, congestion, stomach cramps, bloating, fatigue, gas, diarrhea or constipation, weight loss or weight gain, skin rashes, depression, irritability, confusion, anxiety and other mood changes

Celiac disease can also manifest as an autoimmune response in the skin. Dermatitis Herpetiformis is a gluten-sensitive skin disease. This subgroup of celiac disease can manifest as itchy skin lesions found on the back of the knees, buttocks, elbows, and/or the face.

Celiac Disease: Diagnosis and Treatment

At this time, a medical diagnosis of celiac disease in North America can only be made by a small bowel biopsy. Blood test screening is now commonly indicated by a medical doctor first. There is no known cure for celiac disease yet, however, it can usually (not in all cases) be effectively treated and controlled by strict adherence to a gluten-free diet.

What is the Gluten-Free Diet?

The gluten-free diet is a diet that is absent of all sources of gluten, including hidden sources of gluten. Keep in mind that gluten-free does not mean "carb-free." Gluten-free grains are not free of carbohydrates, therefore, you need to be conscious of that when consuming gluten-free foods. Learning how to live a gluten-free lifestyle requires time, patience and support.

To follow the gluten-free diet properly, one must become educated about which ingredients should be avoided, and which ingredients are safe. It is also important to learn about how to avoid issues of cross-contamination, in order to prevent accidental ingestion of gluten. You can see Kathy's own compilation of "gluten containing" ingredients to avoid in her guide "Kathy's Smart Ingredient Guide" which is available through her website, www.LivetheSmartWay.com. Please see our recommended list of online resources, blogs and books near the end of this e-book for further information and support.

Hidden Sources of Gluten

- Malt is derived from barley which contains gluten

- Hydrolyzed Vegetable/Plant Protein (HVP/HPP) is made from wheat gluten; hydrolysis is the breaking down of protein by acids or enzymes, and most are made from corn, soy or wheat

- Baking Powder contains wheat starch, which contains gluten

- Spices and Seasonings may contain flour if not listed individually on label

- Food Starch/Modified Starch: normally the type of starch is identified; cornstarch can be called starch

- Beers and Ales: distilled alcohol such as gin, vodka, whiskey and rye are acceptable, however, some individuals still react
- Soy sauce and Tamari: some contain wheat
- Processed Foods: sausages, puddings, ice cream, low fat dairy products, canned meat or fish, soups, gravies or sauces, salad dressings, imitation seafood, processed meats, chips; all may use wheat products as fillers
- Dextrin is a starch partially hydrolyzed from any grain, usually from corn or tapioca; used as a thickener or stabilizer
- Many pharmaceutical companies use starch-binding materials in their products which could include wheat starch

How much Gluten can Cause a Problem?

- It only takes 1 gram of gluten for a celiac or gluten sensitive individual to have an outbreak of symptoms!
- That is just one single crumb!

Even just 1/8 of a teaspoon can cause an eruption of symptoms

Did You Know?

- 14,000 allergy-related visits in the last year required 400 hospital stays *
  - Emergency and hospital visits cost Canadians over $5 million per year *
- The direct and indirect economic burden of food allergy/gluten reactions to Canadian households managing these conditions exceeds $5 billion per year*
  - 12% of allergic/gluten reactions need to be treated in emergency rooms *

* Source: Canadian Celiac Association , January 24, 2011

Gluten-Free Certification

If you have gluten-intolerance, it is important to be aware of the fact that although dining establishments and food companies may make claims of their products being gluten-free, there is always a risk of cross-contamination.

Some companies have gluten-free certification for their products. That means that such companies receive gluten-free certification from associations and organizations (generally non-profit) that have programs in place with strict standards (you should verify the level of standards depending on the program in question) for what is considered gluten-free; they inspect products for gluten, and as a result, provide certification to businesses for their products where appropriate.

For example, the Gluten Intolerance Group (also known as GIG) manages a program called "Gluten-Free Certification Organization" or GFCO which does exactly that. The Canadian Celiac Association (which is also non-profit) manages Canada's Gluten-Free Certification Program (GFCP).

The goal of these programs is to strengthen identification of gluten-free products, public safety and consumer confidence. Usually if a product has gluten-free certification, a certification logo will be indicated on the product packaging. It is a good idea to be aware of the programs and logos that are considered safe.

We do not endorse any particular gluten-free certification programs.

For more information about gluten-free certification, you can visit:

http://www.gluten.net/gfco/default.aspx

http://www.celiac.ca/index.php/about-the-cca/certification/

Gluten-Free Grains

Cavena Nuda (Naked Oats)

– A new gluten-free grain introduced to the public in 2009

- Also known as Rice of the Prairies, Cavena Nuda is a hull-less, gluten-free oat grain that when cooked can be a replacement to brown rice, wheat berries or quinoa. It has a chewy texture with amazing nutritional benefits - just ¼ cup has 5 grams of fibre and 8 grams of protein!

- Cavena, meaning Canadian Naked Oats, is the culmination of decades of research by "Dr. Oats," Dr. Vern Burrows and Agriculture Canada

- Cavena is unique, as the oat itself is naturally both hull-less and hairless. There is no difference in the look or growth of the plant until harvest. When cavena is threshed, the hull is removed and returned to the soil immediately, where it breaks down, improving the health of the field. Cavena is then much moredense, needing far less storage space and hauling, reducing the carbon footprint. While regular oats need heat treating once the hull is removed, Cavena has natural defences against spoiling.

Cavena offers excellent nutritional qualities:

- **High Beta Glucan Levels** - The high levels of beta glucan in Cavena means that it can lower your cholesterol levels, improving your cardiovascular system without the use of drugs or artificial supplements.
- **Wheat-Free** - Cavena can offer a new source of nutrition for those who are gluten intolerant or celiac
- **High Protein** - Cavena has a very easily digested protein content, with very high levels of lysine - the key to good muscle growth. Because it is not heat treated, it retains all of its protein until eaten (Smart and Natural Foods Ltd., 2012, www.mysmartfoods.com)

Amaranth

- Amaranth is not an actual grain; it is an ancient Aztec plant which produces flowerets containing tiny grain-like seeds

- It has a nut-like flavor, is high in protein, and is the second highest in quality protein (second only to quinoa, being short of lysine to be a complete protein), dietary fiber, iron, magnesium, phosphorus, potassium, zinc, calcium and B vitamins.

- Excellent added to baked goods in addition to other gluten-free flours

Buckwheat

- Buckwheat is classified as a fruit, not a cereal grain, and is closely related to rhubarb. It is triangular in shape, and has a black shell. The kernel inside the shell is known as a groat. Groats, or dehulled buckwheat kernels are sold roasted or unroasted. Roasted groats are called kasha; roasting gives buckwheat kernels a nutty flavor.

- Unroasted whole groats are cooked and used as a side dish, pasta (soba noodles), or can be ground into cream of buckwheat cereal or flour

- This flour is excellent when added to other gluten-free flours in order to add a nutty and robust taste

Coconut Flour

- Made from ground coconut meat

- Excellent high-fiber alternative to wheat

- Coconut flour can be used to make breads, cakes, pies and other baked goods. Use 15 – 25% in place of other flours in standard recipes, or use 100% coconut flour to create a variety of delicious goods by following specially formulated recipes.

- For each portion of coconut flour used, add an equal amount of additional liquid in the form of water, or double your eggs to give your baked goods a nicer gluten-free consistency

- It has the highest fibre content of any flour. Having a very low concentration of digestible carbohydrates makes it an excellent choice for those who must restrict their carbohydrate intake.

Garfava Flour

- Garfava flour is blended from a combination of chickpeas and fava (or broad beans), and it is high in protein and fiber

- Garfava Flour improves the texture of cakes, cookies, muffins, bagels, scones, and even pizza crust; its mild, nutty flavor makes for great tortillas as well!

Garbanzo Flour

- Garbanzo flour is ground chickpeas, and it is high in protein and fiber

- Use up to 25% bean flour in your gluten-free flour mix to add protein, fiber, and iron

- Use bean flour to thicken or cream soups, stews, sauces and gravies

Millet

- Millet is a cereal commonly used in Europe, and is gaining popularity in North America. It is one of the oldest of the ancient grains. Millet contains considerable protein, as well as B vitamins, lecithin, calcium, iron, magnesium, phosphorus and potassium.

- Millet is an excellent addition to soups and stews, to thicken and add creaminess without the added flour or cream

Potato Flour/Starch

- Potato flour is coarser than potato starch. It is creamy and heavy in texture. It absorbs much more liquid than potato starch. Potato four is best combined in small quantities with other flours. Potato starch is an excellent thickener, and can be used in baking.

Corn

- Corn was first grown in North America, and continues to be the most widely used grain in this hemisphere. When used in rotation with other grains, it is an important nutrient because it is the only grain which contains vitamin A

- Corn is ground into cornmeal, which has a coarser texture than corn flour

- Corn flour and cornmeal are both excellent used in combination with other gluten-free flours for quick breads

Rice

- A staple food for more than half of the world's people, rice comes in long, medium and short grain varieties.

- Brown rice has the indigestible husk removed, but still has the whole kernel, and is rich in nutrients such as B vitamins, vitamin E, iron, protein and linoleic acid (omega-6 fatty acids)

- Add brown rice flour to baked goods, sauces, gravies or stews to thicken, and add texture without added gluten

Wild Rice

- Wild rice, an aquatic grass indigenous to North America, grows extensively in shallow lakes and streams

- It is not a member of the rice family, and has a distinct, nut-like, roasted flavor. It is a good source of dietary fiber and protein, and is a source of phosphorus, potassium and zinc

Rice Bran

- Made from the hulls of brown rice. It has a high concentration of minerals and B vitamins

- Rice bran is an incredible source of the vitamins, minerals, amino acids, essential fatty acids and antioxidant nutrients that help fight disease and promote good health. It's no wonder the healthy oil that comes from rice bran is becoming so successful at replacing hydrogenated oils containing trans-fat. Research is on-going with this invaluable food source, and scientists have found components critical to human health.

Sorghum

- Sorghum is a major cereal grain that grows in hot, semi-arid tropical, and dry temperate areas of the world (USA, Mexico, Africa, India, and China)

- It is similar in composition to corn. Sorghum is a good source of protein and dietary fiber, and is high in phosphorus, potassium, B1, B3, B6 and iron.

- Sorghum is an excellent gluten-free flour to add to baked goods

- Add ½ to 1 Tablespoon of corn starch to every cup of sorghum flour to improve smoothness and moisture retention

Tapioca Starch/Tapioca flour

- Both are made from the cassava root that has been processed, dehydrated and finely ground to create a very fine powder (they are the same thing)

- Excellent used as a thickener for sauces and gravies

Teff

- Teff is a grass native to Ethiopia and the eastern African highlands, and is the smallest of all grains in the world

- This grain is used to make "injera," which is flat, thin, porous bread. It has a unique, mild molasses-like flavor, and the grain can be white or black. Teff seeds are more nutritious than most grains, as the small seed size means the germ and bran (the outer part of the seed) account for a much larger volume of the seed, and these portions are where the nutrients are concentrated. Teff is high in protein, calcium, magnesium, iron, B1, B2, B3 and zinc.

- Teff can also be used as a thickener in soups, gravies and stews

Whole Bean Flour

- Whole bean flour is made from romano beans

- It is high in protein and dietary fiber, and provides more calcium, iron, potassium, B1, B2, and folate than other traditional gluten-free fours

- Baked products made with bean flours have a better texture that more closely resembles wheat products, however, the flavor will be different

Oats

- The safety of oats in individuals with celiac disease has been extensively investigated. Clinical evidence confirms that consumption of pure, uncontaminated oats is safe in the amount of 50 to 70 grams per day (½ – ¾ cup dry rolled oats) by adults, and 20 to 25 grams per day (¼ cup dry rolled oats) by children with celiac disease (Canadian Celiac Association, 2007).

- Studies looking at the consumption of oats over five years have confirmed their safety. However, the studies looking at safety of oats in celiac disease have involved a small number of subjects, the oats used were pure, free of gluten contamination, and the amount allowed per day was also limited (Canadian Celiac Association, 2007). More research is needed to better confirm the safety of oats in individuals with celiac disease.

Gluten-Free Seeds

Chia Seeds

- A 1-ounce serving of chia (salvia hispanica L) contains approximately 4.9 grams of omega 3 fatty acids. Comparatively, flaxseed, which is another good plant source of omega 3 fatty acids, supplies about 1.8 grams of omega 3 fatty acids in a 1-ounce serving. Chia seeds are excellent when added to breads or gluten-free cereals in order to increase the fiber and Omega 3 fatty acids that are often lacking in a gluten-free diet.

- A 1-ounce serving of chia seeds contain 4.4 grams of protein. Compare that to a 1-ounce serving of kidney beans, which supply .01 grams of protein. As you can see, ounce per ounce, chia seeds are a concentrated source of nutrition.

Flaxseeds

- Flax is rich in alpha-linolenic acid, an essential omega-3 fatty acid, a source of dietary fiber and plant lignans

- Flaxseeds may help protect against coronary heart disease, osteoporosis, as well as breast and colon cancer

- Add ground flax to porridge, cereal, gluten-free breads, pasta or yogurt to increase the fiber content, and to improve texture and elasticity

Quinoa

- Quinoa contains more protein than any other grain; an average of 16.2 percent, compared with 7.5 percent for rice, 9.9 percent for millet, and 14 percent for wheat

- Quinoa's protein is of an unusually high quality. It is a complete protein, with an essential amino acid balance close to the ideal, similar to milk.

- Quinoa is an excellent gluten-free alternative to couscous or barley, and can be used in recipes interchangeably

- Quinoa seeds are naturally covered with saponin, an extremely bitter resin which protects it from birds and insects. To be edible, the saponin must be removed. It has been consumed for thousands of years in South America, originating from the Andean Mountains, and was one of the staple foods of the Inca civilization. Quinoa contains the highest amount of protein, and the highest quality protein compared to any other grain or cereal, as it is a complete protein containing all essential amino acids. It is also high in iron, magnesium, phosphorus, potassium, zinc, B1, B2, B3, calcium and dietary fiber.

- Quinoa's protein is high in lysine, methionine and cystine. This makes it an excellent food to combine with, and boost the protein value of other grains (which are low in lysine), or soy (which is low in methionine and cystine).

Gluten-Free Gums

- Guar Gum is made from a seed native to tropical Asia. The guar seeds are dehusked, milled and screened to obtain the guar gum. It is usually produced as a free-flowing, pale, off-white-colored, coarse to finely ground powder. Xantham gum is made by a micro-organism called Xanthomonas Camestris. Both of these gums are used in gluten-free cooking to bind and thicken the finished product. Without adding these gums, baking products are often very dry and crumble easily.

- Xanthan Gum is preferred for baked goods like cookies and breads. Guar Gum is best for cold foods like sorbets, ice creams and pastry fillings. Foods with citrus content can cause guar gum to lose its thickening ability. For recipes that use citrus, use xanthan gum, or use double the amount of guar gum requested. To ensure that the gums dissolve properly, ensure you add the gums to the oil component of the recipe to make a complete mix.

Gluten-Free Baking Tips

When baking gluten-free, it's important to know that you cannot effectively replace all-purpose wheat flour with one type of gluten-free flour alone. Ideally, you need a gluten-free flour, starch flour, and gum combination as a more suitable replacement. Flour blends that are high in starch produce better quality baked goods. Flour blends that include bean flours produce baked goods that are moist and less crumbly than other gluten-free flour combinations. Be careful not to over-bake or over-cook. If your gluten-free flour falls apart when you roll it out for cookies or other baked goods, simply pinch it back together.

Bibliography

Gluten-Free Diet, Shelley Case, BSc, RD

Women's Bodies, Women's Wisdom, Dr. Christine Northrup

Eat Fat, Lose Fat, Dr. Mary Enig and Sally Fallon

Nourishing Traditions, Sally Fallon and Mary G. Enig, Ph.D.

Nutrition Almanac, Sixth Edition, JohnD. Kirschmann and Nutrition Search Inc.

Prescription for Dietary Wellness, Phylliss A. Balch, CNC

The Hormone Diet, Dr. Natasha Turner

Ecoholic, Adria Vasil

Canadian Celiac Association www.celiac.ca

Foundation Quebecoise de la Maladie www.fqmc.org

Weston A. Price Foundation www.westonaprice.org

Resources

Canadian Celiac Association www.celiac.ca

Gluten-Free Certification Organization www.gfco.org

Canadian Celiac Association Website for Health Professionals and Consumers www.celiacguide.org

Bob's Redmill Natural Food Inc., www.bobsredmill.com

El Peto Products www.elpeto.com

Avena www.onlyoats.ca

Food For Life www.foodforlife.com

Go Go Quinoa www.gogoquinoa.com

Ontario Natural Food Co Op www.ofc.ca

Community Supported Agrculture www.csafarms.ca

www.wheatbellyblog.com

www.glutenfreefind.com